Travels in the Holy Land

Shrine to the god Pan at Banias

Travels in the Holy Land

Richard Hughes

MEREHURST PRESS
LONDON

Published 1989 by Merehurst Press, Ferry House,
51-57 Lacy Road, Putney, London SW15 1PR

Co-Published in Australia and New Zealand by
Child and Associates
5 Skyline Place, French's Forest
Sydney 2086,
Australia

ISBN 1 85391 039 2

Designed and produced by Snap! Books

Printed in Great Britain by Butler and Tanner Ltd,
Frome, Somerset

Typeset by Maggie Spooner Typesetting
Illustrations by Millree
Maps by Sue Lawes
Cover illustration: Pilgrims approaching Jerusalem
by David Roberts. By kind permission of Royal
Holloway and Bedford New College, Egham,
Surrey/Bridgeman Art Library.

Contents

Author's Preface

Two thousand years ago the southern part of the province of Syria was called Palestina by imperial Rome, a title detested by the Jews because it associated the land with the hated Philistines of old. The name has survived nevertheless — for John Betjeman the source of an evocative rhyme:

. . . God was Man in Palestine
And lives to-day in Bread and Wine.

But for some people, the name remains controversial. In political terms, the land west of the Jordan is controlled by the state of Israel and the name Palestine is related to the Arab cause. Yet a name acceptable to all can be found — because the region is holy to three great world religions. Jew, Christian and Muslim alike agree that this is the Holy Land. It explains the title of this book, *Travels in the Holy Land*. No country has haunted the imagination so much as this, and few can boast so long or so remarkable a history.

In my first experience of it, I hitched a ride with a B.B.C. team preparing a series of television programmes for schools entitled 'Background to the Gospels'. The magical letters B.B.C. opened doors. One eminent Israeli scholar invited us to visit 'a mouse' (it turned out to be Emmaus). And a British archaeologist led us nonchalantly through a battlefield of the Six Day War in the Judean wilderness, looking for the remains of the palace fortress of Herod the Great called Hyrcania. I am not recommending that route. Live bullets were lying around everywhere, with the remains of wire-guided missiles and shiny anti-personnel mines in blue and silver.

Yet I would not have missed that visit to Hyrcania — in many ways it epitomized the Holy Land. History is writ large there on the face of the desert. As the discoverers of the Dead Sea Scrolls found out, the Judean wilderness is one of the world's dry stores preserving antiquities as practically nowhere else on earth. Although the visit took place in the early spring, the desert was already shimmering in heat — a gigantic, untidy bedspread of ochre rock and sand. We drove towards the remains of Herod's fortress in a battered Renault saloon, skirting the wreckage of Jordanian tanks and armoured cars destroyed by the Israelis in 1967. In the distance, we could see the high mound on which Hyrcania had been built — the centre of King Herod's secret police. The place had an evil reputation. In the first century B.C., people taken to Hyrcania for questioning were never seen again.

We saw a modern war, but we also saw an ancient war. In A.D. 66, seventy years after Herod's death, a violent Jewish revolt broke out against the power of Rome. No history books record the zealot occupation of Hyrcania during the suppression of the Jewish revolt. Yet around the remains of it over nineteen centuries later we found the remains also of square Roman forts lying in the desert, built when the legions laid seige to the zealots defending Hyrcania, probably in A.D. 68.

There was even more to see when we arrived at the fortress itself. The climb to the ruins about five hundred feet above involved a scramble over high boulders and rocks. We saw the defensive walls of Hyrcania, made up of massive slabs of dressed stone. Within them were the paved courtyards and the stunted walls of many buildings from the time of Herod the Great. But there was also evidence of quite different activities in the ruins of the fortress. Byzantine mosaics, depicting brightly coloured flowers and birds, lay there neglected and derelict in the sand. And we found a mausoleum cut into the rock, the uneven plastered walls decorated with the frescoes of saints. The bones of ancient monks were exposed, bleached by more than a thousand years of the Judean sun. I knew little of this period at the time. But soon after, I went to the library to find out. St Sabas had come here in A.D. 492, in search of a solitary retreat where he could spend Lent. Hyrcania was known as Castellium in his time and was, according to the local shepherds, a haunt of demons.

St Cyril of Scythopolis, in his biography of Sabas, gives a dramatic account of what happened. The saint sprinkled the ruins of Castellium with oil of the Holy Cross, and stayed there in the face of all demonic powers. After a supreme effort against his prayers, 'the demons left at midnight, with a tremendous din like a multitude of crows'. After Easter, the Saint returned with other monks to establish a community of hermits at Castellium.

Part of the art of tourism is to know what a country has to offer. It is a prerequisite of a visit to France, for instance, that the traveller should enjoy good conversation — aided and abetted by good food and wine. There are many other things in France, but these are of the essence. Nor can a visit to Greece be complete without a heightened sense of the beauty and significance of humanity — reflected in the classical sculpture, architecture and much else. When it come to such evaluations, the Holy Land too has its own unique perspectives to offer — illustrated supremely well at Hyrcania. Greece is a temple to the human mind and the human body, but the Holy Land has accumulated and has preserved for us the ages. This is a crucible of civilization.

Nowhere are the secrets of archaeology hidden in such profusion as here. The past of jostling humanity can be found in the soil and the sands of the Holy Land. Few countries can boast so long or so interesting a past — a story on the one hand of human savagery and atrocity, on the other of the profoundest of spiritual perceptions. Herod the Great's secret police used Hyrcania as a prison, the zealots made it into a desert retreat, but Sabas made Castellium into a spiritual sanctuary in the wilderness. A list of the rulers of the Holy Land from Solomon to Suleiman the Magnificent reads like a 'Who's Who' of oriental despots. But the Holy Land also leads us to a list of great spiritual leaders from Elijah to Christ, from Peter the fisherman to Muhammad the prophet. The history of the Holy Land describes humanity both at its worst and at its best — as will be evident again and again during the course of these ten days of travel in the land of the Bible.

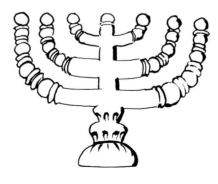

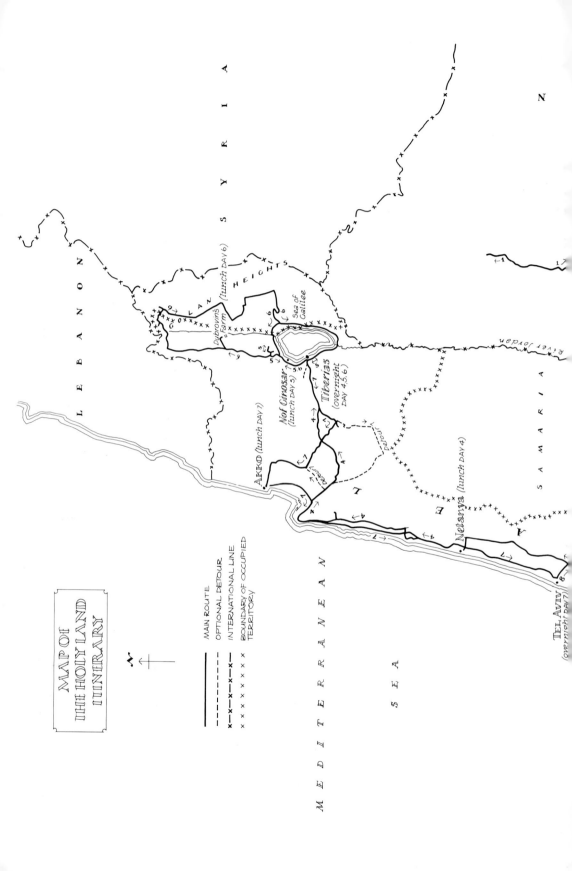

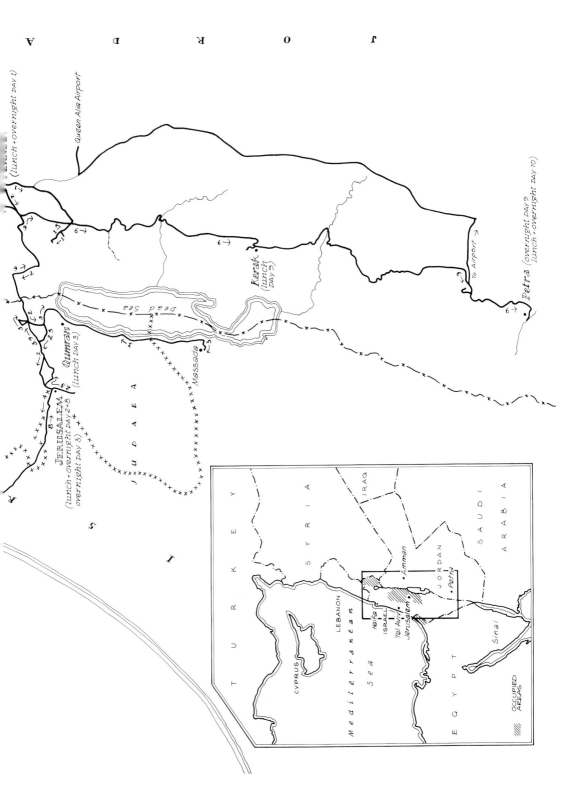

The Hanging Palaces at Masada

Introduction
to the
Holy Land

Al-Jazzar Mosque, Acre

Geography

In the early Old Testament period this was the Land of Canaan — a country which extended, so it was said, 'from Dan to Beersheba'. It included territories now found in the State of Israel, the occupied West Bank and the mountains of Gilead in the Hashemite Kingdom of Jordan. To the south of Gilead lay the neighbouring ancient kingdoms of Moab and Edom. To the east was Ammon, while the Aramean kingdoms of Syria lay to the north — at different times, the Israelites fought all the surrounding nations.

For the most part, the biblical names are as valid today as in the past and can be used for a modern geographical description — although there are many variants in their spelling, and over so long a history placenames have changed from time to time and are still changing. Such changes will be noted in this book when necessary and cross-referenced in the index. The ancient city of Akko, for instance, is also spelled Accho or Acco. It was called Ptolemais in New Testament times, and Acre by the Crusaders. Akko was first built by the Phoenicians long before biblical times on one of the few natural harbours of the Mediterranean seaboard, see p. 119.

The most striking physical feature of the Holy Land is the deep rift of the Jordan Valley which extends from the Beqaa Valley in the Lebanon to the Gulf of Aqaba in the south. It is one of the deepest gashes in the face of the earth — 683 ft below sea level at the Sea of Galilee, and 1306 ft below sea level at the Dead Sea. This is part of a much larger geological fault, the northern extremity of the Great East African Rift Valley which extends as far south as Lake Tanganyika.

To a large extent the other physical features of the Holy Land run from north to south parallel to the rift valley. The transjordanian plateau east of the rift is incised with deep wadis. (*Wadi* is a term used in the region — it describes a river valley frequently dry in this climate.) The Samaritan hills west of the Jordan form the central watershed of the Holy Land. The land rises steeply from the base of the valley — about 3000 ft in nine miles. This West Bank territory is a land of dramatic contrasts. Precipitous barren slopes tower above deep ravines where tall cypresses and luxuriant meadows are watered by innumerable springs. In the south, the watershed descends to Jerusalem and the Judean hill country beyond. In the north, the Carmel Range and the flat table land of Jezreel cut east-west across the main geographical structures. But the pattern returns where the Golan Heights hang over the deep basin of the Upper Jordan Valley. In most parts of the Holy Land, sheep and goats constitute the flocks — only in the Golan are cattle found in large numbers.

West of the central spine of the Holy Land lies the great strip of the coastal plain, extending from the Plain of Akko in the north to the Negev in the south, interrupted only by the Carmel Range. In ancient times, most of this land was a mosquito-ridden swamp. But now the coastal plain is rich in orchards of orange, grapefruit and lemon, fish tanks, and fields of cotton, tobacco, wheat and maize. The coast itself is punctuated with a string of popular holiday resorts — such as Netanya, see p. 82-3.

Until recent years, the Negev in the south was largely desert. But the effects of the systematic irrigation of this land over the last thirty years can be seen. Extended rows of tomatoes, peppers and aubergines stretch in the western Negev so far as the eye can see, irrigated by waterpipes laid along the roads and through the fields. With the addition of water, the desert is astonishingly fertile. The large-scale taking of water from the River Jordan for irrigation has, however, considerably lowered the level of the Dead Sea.

South of the Judean hill country, the desert finally takes over. The desert hills in this region are orientated northeast-southwest, and lead to the dramatic mountain ranges of the Sinai. The State of Israel extends through the desert as far south as Eilat on the Gulf of Aqaba — a busy port and popular holiday resort. As well as hotels and crowded beaches, there is a nature reserve at Eilat and a fascinating underwater observatory of marine life. A new airport to serve the resort has been built in the desert to the north.

Archaeology

This book is about the Holy Land, an area which crosses modern national boundaries, but the story of civilization in this extraordinary and beautiful country begins with city states rather than with nations. And to comprehend it requires a readjustment of our timescales, since the ancient cities of the Holy Land make even the Old Testament seem quite recent. As the psalmist reflects:

> For a thousand years in thy sight are but as yesterday: seeing that it is past as a watch in the night.

The earliest biblical history tells of the entry of Abraham into the Land of Canaan, probably in the eighteenth century B.C. But the Israelites did not arrive in force until after their escape from Egypt and their profound religious experiences in the wilderness of the Sinai. According to the Bible, the walls of Jericho fell down miraculously on their arrival. But Jericho was already eight thousand years old when the Israelites arrived, probably in the mid-thirteenth century B.C. — less than three and a half thousand years ago. It illustrates very well the readjustments to be made. The Israelite invasion took place at about the time when the people of Britain were busily putting the finishing touches to Stonehenge.

But why did the civilizations of the Middle East develop so much earlier? The answer seems to be trade. Merchants with their trains of pack mules and camels carried goods from one place to another. Writing was invented so that people could make out stock lists and invoices. And the development of cities owed much to the trade routes — because those routes also beat a path for invading armies. Isolated settlements became too vulnerable. The time came when people lived in cities surrounded by strong walls, manned by swordsmen and archers, a refuge in time of war for people living in the surrounding villages.

But did the walls of ancient Jericho really fall down? The archaeologists can show no evidence to support the Bible story. It rains heavily in the winter months in the Lower Jordan Valley, and the remains of the last Canaanite city at Jericho have long been washed away. Nor can archaeology provide solutions to many of our other questions. Archaeologists find only such signs of human habitation as artifacts which were lost, thrown away or placed in tombs and the remains of walls and houses, shrines and burial places. The significance of their finds can be extrapolated to give an impression of what life in the past was like. But even an intensive study of a site can provide no more than tantalizing glimpses of the various stages of civilization which existed there. Yet as will be seen in the course of these travels, remarkable archaeological discoveries have been made in the Holy Land. And more will undoubtedly come to light. The land of the Bible is littered with the sites of ancient cities, many of them as yet untouched by the archaeologists — few indeed have been thoroughly excavated.

It is relatively easy to recognize the sites of the ancient cities — the remains of them rise high above the surrounding countryside. Early settlements were built near springs, most of them on mounds because such sites were more easily defensible. Since the ordinary domestic buildings and most of the other structures in these cities were constructed of mudbrick, the site rose higher by a few inches in each century as old buildings were knocked down and new ones were built.

These mounds are called 'tels'; many stand over seventy feet high above the surrounding countryside, the debris of thousands of years of human habitation — a veritable human ant heap. In order to examine the successive strata of civilization, it is usual for the archaeologists to cut a section, or several sections, into a tel as the diagram shows.

The Ancient Trade Routes

The Way of the Sea, so called in the Old Testament, was an important trade and military route which ran from Canaanite until Roman times the whole length of the Holy Land from north to south. Merchants plied this road from city to city, buying in one market and selling in another. And this was also the path of warring armies — at times from Egypt in the southwest, at other times from Anatolia, Assyria, Babylonia or Persia in the northeast. The Holy Land was a corridor through which the conquering armies of the ancient world passed in turn. On the northern part of the Way of the Sea lay the most important trading city of the Middle East in pre-biblical times, Hazor, on the Rosh Pinna Sill north of the Sea of Galilee, see p. 102. Further south the main

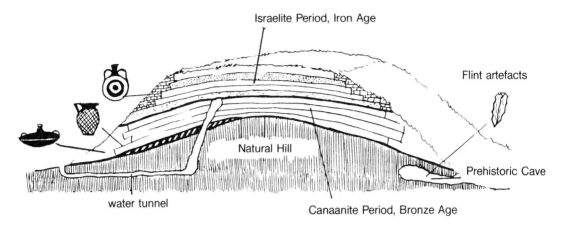

Cross-section of a tel.

Since pottery is non-biodegradable, it survives in large quantities and helps date the strata of a tel.

route was joined at Megiddo by a secondary branch of the Way of the Sea which ran south from the Lebanese coast. No city wielded as much control as Megiddo over the Way of the Sea. After leaving the valley of Jezreel, the road entered the narrow confines of the Iron Pass dominated by Megiddo.

Once through the Pass, the Way of the Sea headed south in the direction of Egypt. But it did not, even then, run near the sea — because the coastal plain of the Holy Land was a malarial swamp. Instead, the road hugged the edges of the hills and ran along the coast only after reaching the desert south of Gaza. After thousands of years of usage, the Way of the Sea was finally abandoned in the Roman period with the building by King Herod the Great of the new port called Caesarea Maritima, see p. 83. From then on, the way to Egypt — and for that matter to any number of other places — was by sea.

The King's Highway was the other major route, complementary to the Way of the Sea, which played an important part in the history of the Holy Land. The King's Highway ran south from Damascus across the transjordanian plateau to Amman — called Rabbah of the Ammonites in the Bible. The road then traversed the Madeba Plateau and moved through the Wadi Mujib and the

Wadi Hasa east of the Dead Sea. The terrain became increasingly rugged as the road gradually approached its final destination at Aqaba. As with the Way of the Sea, the King's Highway was little more than a rough track along which merchants with their pack camels and mules regularly plied, visiting the city markets along the way. From Aqaba, goods were taken by sea along the coasts of Arabia and East Africa.

This too was a path of warring armies. The road is associated in particular with a military expedition described in Genesis 14. Four marauding kings from the north travelled this route in the eighteenth century B.C., taking one city after another and exacting tribute. After Aqaba they travelled the desert road through the Sinai to the oasis at Qadesh Barnea. The kings then turned east once more, and descended into the Valley of the Dead Sea — called the Valley of Siddim in Genesis. One of the aims of the expedition was to gather bitumen from the Dead Sea to caulk their boats — probably harboured at Tyre, the greatest port on the Mediterranean at the time. But the arrival of the kings did not go unopposed. In a bitter battle on the shores of the Dead Sea, they fought and defeated the combined forces of five local kings. Some of their opponents perished in the bitumen pits of the Dead Sea, while others fled into the hills. Genesis tells us that as part of their booty the kings of the north took hostage Abraham's nephew Lot and his family. It explains the relevance of the history of the four kings to the Bible narrative.

When Abraham heard of the capture of Lot, he was able to rouse three hundred and eighteen of his kinsmen to go in pursuit. The four kings now followed the Way of the Sea on their journey north. They were encamped in the Upper Jordan Valley when Abraham and his kinsmen descended on them. In a fierce encounter, Abraham released Lot and his family and chased the remains of the marauding army to Hobah beyond Damascus.

This story is revealing for a number of reasons. Most of the biblical accounts of Abraham were passed on for centuries by word of mouth before being written down. In them the patriarch is described as a solitary shepherd with his wife, his family and his flocks of sheep and goats. But Genesis 14 is one of the earliest pieces of near-contemporary reporting in the Old Testament — and Abraham is shown as an important tribal chieftain able to raise at short notice a powerful band of kinsmen to defeat his enemies. The transjordanian road is called the King's Highway to this day because this route is associated with the expedition of the kings of the north described in Genesis 14.

While the Way of the Sea and the King's Highway were the major routes, many minor roads also played their part in the history of the Holy Land. Various tracks ran through the central hill country, for instance, their use illustrated in the biblical narrative when Joseph was sold at Dothan by his brothers to Ishmaelite traders on the way from Gilead to Egypt. Other minor trade routes ran through the mountains of Upper Galilee, linking the Phoenician ports at Tyre and Akko to the Upper Jordan Valley. A road also ran south from the Sea of Galilee to Jericho, through the oppressive heat of the Jordan valley. As with the major trade routes, these roads were also used from time to time for military purposes.

History

This is a history of war. The Holy Land lay on a corridor between the great powers of the ancient world. The Pharoah Pepi I marched north on the Way of the Sea into what he called the 'land of the Sand-dwellers' in 2350 B.C. — the earliest known of many military expeditions to impose Egyptian power in the Land of Canaan. Later, the rulers of Anatolia or the Mesopotamian valley followed that same road, attracted south by the rich cities of Egypt. And the great trading cities of the Holy Land — Hazor, for instance, or Lachish — were built on or near the Way of the Sea. Only Jerusalem, which was to become a holy city, was hidden in the hills, surrounded by deep ravines and protected by precipitous mountain slopes.

The Bronze Age, Canaanites and Phoenicians
c. 3150-1200 B.C.

History emerges from prehistory in the Holy Land with the great Canaanite and Phoenician cities of the Bronze Age — such as Hazor, see p. 102. During this period many other small tribes, such as the Jebusites, also flourished in the Holy Land, while other nations such as the Ammonites, subsisted on the borders. The art of writing had been developed in the Mesopotamian valley long before, but civilization is indebted to the Canaanites for the invention of alphabetic script — between twenty and thirty signs instead of the vast number used in earlier writing systems.

The Israelite Period, c. 1350-722 B.C.

The Israelites arrived in the mid-thirteenth century B.C. after years of wandering the vast rugged wilderness of the Sinai. At about the same time, the Philistines established themselves in the south of the coastal plain — their cities were Ashdod, Ashqelon, Gaza, Ekron and Gath. These were the Sea Peoples — immigrants from the Aegean. The Old Testament tells of battles between the Philistines and the Israelites during the time of Saul, the first Israelite king who was defeated and killed by them. His successor, King David, ruled an Israelite empire which extended from Aqaba to the banks of the Euphrates. But his son Solomon taxed the people heavily to pay for massive building projects — including the Temple at Jerusalem. After his reign, the northern tribes broke away from the Kingdom of Judah and formed a separate Kingdom of Israel. The two kingdoms fought the surrounding nations and also regularly fought each other.

The Assyrian Period, 722-628 B.C.

The armies of successive Assyrian monarchs descended on the Holy Land. The Kingdom of Israel became an Assyrian province — only Judah survived. Members of the northern tribes were deported to other parts of the Assyrian empire and were replaced with peoples of other origins. Intermarriage between the natives and the newcomers gave rise to the people known as the Samaritans.

Josiah, 640-609 B.C.

After the decline in Assyrian power, Josiah was able to reunite Israel and Judah for a short period. But he died at Megiddo in 609 B.C., attempting to impede a campaign to the north of the Necoh, the Egyptian pharoah.

The Babylonian Period, 604-538 B.C.

The Babylonians under Nebuchadnezzar II took Jerusalem in 587 B.C. The Temple built by Solomon was destroyed and many important citizens of Judah were taken as slaves into exile in Babylonia.

The Persian Period, 538-332 B.C.

Cyrus, king of Persia, overthrew the power of Babylonia. In 538 B.C., he allowed the Jewish exiles to return to Judah and to begin the task of rebuilding the holy city and its Temple. Later, offers of assistance to rebuild the Temple were made by the Samaritans, and were firmly rejected by the returning exiles. It explains the enmity between the Jews and the Samaritans in New Testament times.

The Hellenistic Period, 332-37 B.C.

Classical Greece was already in decline when, in the wake of the conquests of Alexander the Great, the Greek spirit was spread throughout the eastern world. This was Hellenism. Greek became a universal language, and Greek cities were built everywhere. The high priest at the Temple in Jerusalem in 174 B.C. changed his name from Joshua to Jason — a Greek name instead of a Jewish name. And there were plans to invest the God of Israel with the Greek name 'Zeus'. It led to the fierce Jewish resistance of the war of the Maccabees, recounted in the Apocrypha.

The Roman Period 37 B.C.-A.D. 324

Nor did the style change very much with the coming of the Romans. Imperial Rome had conquered Greece, but the Romans and their adherents cultivated Hellenism. It was said of King Herod the Great, whose reign began in 37 B.C., that his religion was Jewish, his allegiance was to Rome and his lifestyle was Greek. The Galilee of the time of Jesus of Nazareth was part of the Graeco-Roman world.

The Roman period was also marked by successive Jewish revolts against the power of Rome. In A.D. 70 in the wake of the first revolt, the Temple at Jerusalem was destroyed never to be rebuilt. The Islamic Dome of the Rock, see p. 62, now stands where the Altar of Sacrifice once stood. And with the Defeat of the Bar Cochba revolt in A.D. 135, biblical Jerusalem itself was destroyed. A new Roman city called Aelia Capitolina was built in its place. Jews were forbidden to enter the new city.

The Byzantine Period, A.D. 324-638

Aelia was a cosmopolitan pagan city until the accession of Constantine, the first Christian ruler of the Roman empire. In A.D. 330 he made Byzantium his capital in the east, renaming the city Constantinople. The Byzantine period in the Holy Land is marked by desert monasticism and by the building of many fine churches. Constantine himself was responsible for the Church of the Holy Sepulchre in Jerusalem (see p. 63) and the Church of the Nativity at Bethlehem, see p. 128. European pilgrims made the long journey to visit the holy places, and Jerome translated the Bible into Latin in his monastery at Bethlehem. He called his translation the Vulgate — 'the book of the people'. So far as Christianity was concerned, the Byzantine period was the golden age of the Holy Land.

The Early Arab Period, A.D. 638-1099

The spread of Islam by the sword ended the Byzantine world. In A.D. 638 the Caliph Umar I took the holy city. The Great Mosque at Damascus and the Dome of the Rock at Jerusalem were built during the Umayyad dynasty which followed. For the most part, the Islamic rulers were tolerant of Christians living in their midst. But at the beginning of the eleventh century, the Caliph al-Hakim ordered the destruction of the Church of the Holy Sepulchre. Stories of the persecution of Christians in the Holy Land were rife. In 1095, Pope Urban II preached the Crusades at Cleremont in southern France, a message which galvanized medieval Europe.

The Crusader Period, A.D. 1099-1291

The remains of Crusader buildings are among the most imposing in the Holy Land. Yet the Crusades were a violent and murderous failure. Great Crusader states were set up throughout the Levant. But they were short lived. The knights were finally defeated by Saladin in 1187 on a hilltop called the Horns of Hittim above the Sea of Galilee, see p. 114. Afterwards, the Crusader kingdom of Jerusalem gave way once more to Islamic rule. A Crusader presence remained in the Holy Land for a further century, but without regaining control of the holy places.

The Later Arab Period, 1291-1516

The Ayyubid dynasty, drawn from members of Saladin's family, ushered in a period of great stability and prosperity in the Holy Land. But Saladin had included a slave corps in his army. And other Islamic rulers had purchased large numbers of slaves, mostly Turks, to use as troops. In 1250 the tables were turned. A slave dynasty called the Mameluks usurped power. They rid the Levant of the last of the Crusaders, and defeated the Mongols descending from the east. Mameluk power was to last two hundred and fifty years. The rise of the Ottoman Empire began in the fourteenth century, when the Islamic Turks struggled to overthrow Christian Byzantium centred on Constantinople.

The Ottoman Period, 1516-1917

The Holy Land was taken by the Ottoman Sultan Selim I in 1516. His son Suleiman the Magnificent ascended the throne in 1520, surrounded by greater power and wealth than any sultan before or since. It marked the peak of Ottoman grandeur, and in the centuries which followed the empire went into a slow decline. Yet, with varying degrees of effectiveness, an Ottoman administration continued to control the Holy Land until 1917 when General Sir Edmund Allenby took Jeruslaem for the British.

Events Leading to the Present

Jews were forbidden Aelia Capitolina (the renamed, rebuilt Jerusalem) in A.D. 135 — reflecting Roman anger at yet another Jewish revolt against the empire. But the 'diaspora' — the dispersal of the Jewish people — had begun long before. Trade had attracted many Jews away from the Holy Land, and there were Jewish colonies throughout the Graeco-Roman world. They returned in vast numbers for the great festivals at the Temple. This was the 'promised land' no matter where they lived — at the heart of their religion and irreplaceable in their affections.

But many religious Jews could not bring themselves to leave the Holy Land, despite sometimes great persecution. And throughout the centuries, Jews returned to the Holy Land in search of spiritual renewal. It is virtually impossible to quantify the Jewish presence in the Holy Land at any given time. But there were always Jews saying their prayers and studying the scriptures in the land of the Old Testament.

The end of the nineteenth century witnessed a great influx of Jewish refugees from eastern Europe. The minority of religious Jews living in the Holy Land at that time were not interested in political achievement — they awaited the coming of the Messiah. But the newcomers had more practical ambitions. Their object was to work the land with their own hands, literally building a Jewish state in the promised land. Nor was the political will lacking elsewhere. The World Zionist Organization was launched at Basle in Switzerland in 1897 to facilitate Jewish nationalism.

In 1922, in the wake of Allenby's campaign, Britain was mandated by the League of Nations to rule Palestine. By this time, the scene was set for a struggle between Arab and Jew for possession of the Holy Land — a conflict which the British found increasingly difficult to resolve as time went by.

The State of Israel

A resolution of the United Nations in 1948 finished the British Mandate, partitioned Palestine and established the State of Israel. Great sympathy was felt for the Jewish people in the wake of their sufferings at the hands of Nazi Germany in World War II. But the creation of the new state dispossessed three quarters of a million Palestinians of their homes. From all sides, the surrounding Arab nations sent in their armies to attack the new state. But they were obliged to cede further lands as they retreated before the Israeli forces.

The Hashemite Kingdom of Jordan

In 1946, Jordan gained independence from the British as a hereditary constitutional monarchy. When the Arab nations went to war in 1948 in an attempt to prevent the formation of the State of Israel, King Abdullah of Jordan used the British-trained Arab Legion to bring half of Jerusalem and the hill country, known as the West Bank, into his kingdom. King Hussein of Jordan came to the throne in 1953. East Jerusalem and the West Bank territories were taken by Israel during the Six Day War in 1967. The River

Jordan now marks the boundary between the Kingdom of Jordan and the West Bank territory occupied by Israel.

The Occupied Territories

A further Arab attempt to overthrow the State of Israel came in 1967. The war lasted only six days. But in that time the Egyptians were thrown back to the Suez canal; the Syrians lost to Israel the Golan Heights and the Jordanians lost East Jerusalem and the West Bank territories. The Sinai peninsula was returned to Egypt as a result of the Camp David agreement in 1979. But the Gaza Strip, the West Bank and the Golan Heights remain occupied by Israel. The Arab inhabitants have few voting rights, nor are they represented in the Israeli Parliament. Many of the West Bank Palestinians continue to live in the insanitary refugee camps set up to receive them in 1948.

Quick Reference to the Historical Periods

The Bronze Age	c. 3150–1200 B.C.
The Israelite Period	c. 1350–722 B.C.
The Assyrian Period	722–628 B.C.
Josiah	640–609 B.C.
The Babylonian Period	604–538 B.C.
The Persian Period	538–332 B.C.
The Hellenistic Period	332–37 B.C.
The Roman Period	37 B.C.–A.D. 324
The Byzantine Period	A.D. 324–638
The Early Arab Period	A.D. 638–1099
The Crusader Period	A.D. 1099–1291
The Later Arab Period	A.D. 1291–1516
The Ottoman Period	A.D. 1516–1917

Food and Drink

Food

The Holy Land abounds in the fresh fruit and vegetables characteristic of both Jordanian and Israeli cuisine. Although the Hashemite Kingdom of Jordan and the State of Israel came into existence only recently, many ancient cultures have contributed to Jordanian and Israeli cooking. Nor should the influence of religion be overlooked. The three great world religions of the Holy Land use food and drink as an expression of faith. There is hardly a single pig farm in the Holy Land, for instance, since pork is proscribed both in Islam and in Judaism — the indignity of the Prodigal Son in Jesus' parable was that he was obliged to look after swine.

The great Jordanian dish is *mensaf* — traditionally a bedouin feast of lamb covered in aromatic herbs and cooked in yoghourt. It is served on layers of rice and wood-cooked bread to guests sitting in a circle around a communal dish. *Mensaf* is associated with weddings, anniversaries and Islamic feasts — an experience rather than simply a meal. It is also a traditional expression of lavish bedouin hospitality or royal largesse. The main meal of the day in Jordan is taken usually at lunch time, and Jordanian cuisine draws recipes from many Middle East sources — stuffed vegetables called *mahshis* are served, for instance, or *fattush*, a traditional salad. Salads consist of black olives, tomatoes, cucumbers and peppers garnished with parsley, mint, tarragon vinegar and olive oil.

Although by no means all the restaurants in Israel are 'kosher', traditional Jewish cooking is governed by the dietary laws of Judaism. The Old Testament injunction that 'you shall not boil a kid in its mother's milk', for instance, is interpreted to mean that meat and milk products should not be served at the same meal — after a meat dish in kosher restaurants milk is not served in coffee. But within these laws, a great variety of different dishes are prepared in Israeli homes and restaurants — since Jews from many different culinary backgrounds now live in the Holy Land. Eastern Europe, for instance, is the origin of the jellied fish so popular in Israel. Casseroles, too, play an important part in Jewish cuisine since a great variety of Sabbath meals are prepared on a Friday for eating on the holy day of rest. Jews originating in Eastern Europe, for instance, might make a slow casserole containing beef, potatoes, beans and barley — whereas Jews from North Africa might prepare the Sabbath casserole with mutton, chickpeas and steamed wheat.

The experience of staying at an Israeli or an Arab hotel resolves many of the problems of eating while on tour in the Holy Land. The 'great Middle East breakfast' means that only a light snack is necessary in the middle of the day. It consists of a large variety of savoury yoghourt products, tomatoes, sardines, cucumbers, boiled eggs and cheese followed by fruit courses. All served with tea or coffee, bread, toast and butter. Milk is almost invariably a dried milk product — cattle are scarce in the Holy Land.

Evening meals at the hotels are usually also substantial, served with hummus, pitta bread and fruit. A great variety of dishes are offered — baked perch, for instance, or lamb and okra stew. Usually there are three courses — soup, a main dish and a dessert.

When travelling and looking for snacks, the best buys at the shops are fruits — oranges, pomegranates, bananas. Biscuits, bread and cooked meats can also be bought. The Jordanian soft drinks are usually very sugary, but the shops also sell international brands, e.g. Coca Cola, Seven-Up.

Pitta Bread

Bread was made every day in the Holy Land in biblical times — it explains the expression 'daily bread' in the Lord's Prayer. Bread from the previous day was hard and leathery — similar to the pitta bread sometimes on sale in English supermarkets.

I saw a vaulted oven suitable for making pitta bread in an underground kitchen in the ruins of Herod the Great's palace fortress at Hyrcania. Wood was burned inside the oven. When the walls were hot, the oven was raked out and used for baking the bread.

1 oz dried yeast
1 tsp sugar
1 lb flour
salt

Mix the dried yeast, sugar and some warm water. When the ingredients have dissolved, stir in the flour and a little salt. Knead the dough for about 10 minutes, then divide into small balls and roll out each till it is rather less than half an inch thick. Cover with a damp cloth and leave for about twenty minutes to rise. Then repeat the process. Place the rolled-out pieces of dough on a well-greased baking tin. Bake for about three minutes, at 240°C/475°F.

Hummus

This chickpea dip is served with most meals in the Middle East.

8 oz chickpeas
juice of 2 lemons
1 clove garlic
2 fl oz tahini
salt, black pepper
paprika
coriander
cumin

Garnish
chopped parsley and olive oil

Hummus cont'd

Boil the chickpeas until soft, then blend in a liquidizer with the lemon juice. Mix in crushed garlic and tahini (sesame-seed paste). Add salt, black pepper, paprika, coriander and cumin to taste. Serve with a garnish of chopped parsley and a little olive oil.

Felafel

4 oz fava beans
4 oz chickpeas
1 clove garlic, crushed
1 small onion, chopped
parsley, chopped
ground coriander
cayenne pepper
ground cumin
bicarbonate of soda
salt, black pepper

Soak dried fava beans in cold water for about 48 hours and the chickpeas for about 12 hours. Mix and liquidize the fava beans and chickpeas, adding crushed garlic and chopped onion. Mix in chopped parsley, ground coriander, cayenne pepper, ground cumin to taste, and a little bicarbonate of soda, salt and black pepper. Shape the mixture into small balls and allow to stand for about 30 minutes. Then cook the balls in hot oil and serve with tomato and lettuce in envelopes of pitta bread.

Blintzes

4 eggs
7 tsp flour
salt
unsalted butter (to fry)

Filling
6 oz cottage cheese
1 lb cream cheese
2 egg yolks

rind of 1 lemon
vanilla essence

Garnish
icing sugar

Combine eggs, flour, about 8 fl oz of water and a little salt and blend in a mixing bowl. Leave in a fridge for several hours. Return the mixture to room temperature and mix again until very smooth. Using unsalted butter for fat, cook the mixture in a pancake until it is lightly browned on both sides.

Blend cottage cheese, cream cheese, egg yolks, lemon rind and vanilla essence to taste. Make envelopes out of the pancakes and fill with the cheese and egg mixture. Then fry the blintzes in butter until they are golden. Serve with a dusting of icing sugar.

Mensaf

You could not easily reproduce the lamb dish served at a typical *mensaf* since the custom is to cook three or four sheep in enormous cooking pots, but the following has something of the flavour and is simple to prepare.

4 fl oz olive oil
2½ lb boned stewing lamb, cubed
5 oz onion, chopped
1 tsp ground cumin
½ tsp salt
½ tsp fresh ground black pepper
8 fl oz stock
8 fl oz natural yoghourt

Garnish
pine kernels, mint leaves and lemon wedges

Heat the oil in a pan and add the lamb, stir until evenly browned. Add onion, cook for a few minutes then add cumin, salt and pepper. Pour in the stock, cover and simmer 1¼ hours. There should be little stock left so take care not to allow it to burn. Remove from the heat and stir in yoghourt. Put in a serving dish decorated with pine kernels, mint leaves and lemon wedges.

Serve with pitta bread or couscous.

Drink

The climate of the Holy Land is ideal for wine-making, and in the nineteenth century Baron Edmond de Rothschild supplied French vines to the Jewish settlers. The Carmel co-operative started by the baron is still the largest maker of wine in the Holy Land. Two other notable sources of wine are the monasteries at Latrun in the Samaritan hill country and at Bethlehem in the Judean hill country. The pleasing red Cremisan wine from Bethlehem is often served as a house-wine. Unlike some Islamic countries, alcoholic drinks are sold in Jordan except during the period of Ramadan. The monasteries at Latrun and Bethlehem supply most of the wine exported for use in Jordanian restaurants.

But the development of the really good wines now available in Israel began after the Golan Heights were captured from the Syrians in the Six Day War of 1967. The volcanic soils and the less sun-baked climate of the Golan offer ideal conditions for viticulture. In 1986 a fine red Cabernet Sauvignon came onto the market under the name Gamla, full-bodied with a pleasant bouquet, likely to improve with the passage of time. In the same year an excellent Sauvignon Blanc under the name Yarden also went on sale. Further types of vine have been planted in recent years, and a greater variety of good quality wines from the Golan can be expected in the future.

It can be argued that one of the main reasons why prehistoric people congregated in settlements was because somebody discovered how to make beer. Certainly, beer-making has gone on in the Middle East since time immemorial. The local brewery in Jordan bottles Amstel beer. In Israel, Carlsberg lager is made under license. But the Israeli Maccabee beer is cheaper, and is of good quality. Spirits in the Holy Land are incredibly expensive — it is worth taking maximum advantage of the 'duty free' shops on entering the country.

A Roman street in the old city of Jerusalem

Useful Information

1. Getting There

TRAVELLING THROUGH THE HOLY LAND
The tour mapped out in this book involves travelling through Jordan and Israel. To visit the eastern parts of the land of the Bible, the visitor must first enter the Hashemite Kingdom of Jordan. Then cross the river into Israel at the Allenby Bridge near Jericho — also called by the Jordanians the King Hussein Bridge. Under present regulations, it is the only place where entry is allowed for visitors passing from the east to the West Bank.

VISA REQUIREMENTS
These travels in the Holy Land begin in the Hashemite Kingdom of Jordan, for which a visa is required. It is possible to obtain a visa on arrival at Queen Alia Airport, Amman or at other points of entry into Jordan. But less time is wasted if the visa is obtained beforehand from a Jordanian Embassy or Consulate. A small charge is made for a visa. To visit Israel no visa is required.

TOURIST FACILITIES
The main tourist organization in Jordan is the Ministry of Tourism and Antiquities, P.O. Box 224, Amman (tel: 642311) — there is an office of the Ministry of Tourism at Queen Alia Airport. Israeli Government Tourist Offices can be found in Jerusalem, but also at 18 Great Marlborough Street, London W1V 1AF (tel: 01 434 3651). The Jordanian Ministry supplies the necessary paper work to allow people to cross to the West Bank. Both tourist offices supply the names of hotels, telephone numbers and answer all kinds of queries about their respective countries.

AIRLINES
Flights are available on most days between London Heathrow and Queen Alia Airport, Amman, operated by the Royal Jordanian Airlines and by British Air. Flying time is about five hours.

It is important to confirm flights with the airline at least 72 hours before flight departure. The visitor should also bear in mind that airport charges are made on departure from Queen Alia Airport.

TIME
The time in Jordan as well as in Israel is Greenwich Mean Time plus two hours.

TOUR OPERATORS
Several tour operators, such as Inter-Church Travel Ltd, 45 Berkeley Street, London W1A 1EB (tel: 01 734 0942), offer package tours of Jordan and the Holy Land. Ramblers' Holidays, Box 43, Welwyn Garden City, Herts AL8 6PQ (tel: 0707 331133), also specialize in cheap flights and accommodation in Jordan and Israel. But to follow this particular itinerary it is probably better to use a local tour operator — such as Guiding Star, 4 Al Hariri Street, PO Box 19421, Jerusalem 91193, Israel (tel: 010 972 2 284019/284231). They also have an office in Amman, and are able to book the necessary accommodation and transport locally. It is important to specify what standard of hotel accommodation is required. If a large party is travelling, the tour operator can also supply transport by coach.

It is essential to book several months in advance, since accommodation and flights are often over-subscribed. Tour operators can obtain cheaper accommodation from a hotel than would be available to an individual enquirer — even people living in the State of Israel often book their holiday accommodation from the tour operators.

CROSSING INTO THE WEST BANK
To cross the Allenby/King Hussein Bridge, the visitor needs the appropriate documents from the Ministry of Tourism at Amman. These can be arranged by the visitor or the tour operator and should be booked at least a week in advance. Entry and exit charges are made at the bridge by the Israeli authorities.

CAR HIRE

It is probably better to hire a taxi or travel by coach for excursions in Jordan. Taxis are not much more expensive than hire cars, and self-drive can present considerable problems. Roadsigns are often in Arabic only — difficult to read for anyone unfamiliar with the language. And to visit places off the usual tourist track — such as Machaerus, p. 136, involves driving through a maze of little roads. There are also the obvious dangers involved in driving through desert areas in a car unknown to you.

There are, however, real advantages to hiring a car when it comes to Israel and the West Bank. The road system is reasonably good, distances are short and roadsigns are almost universally in Hebrew, Arabic and English. It is possible to reserve a hire car in advance from most of the international car hire companies. For the itinerary mapped out in this book I recommend you hire a car for 6 days to be collected in Jerusalem on Day 3 of your trip.

2. On Tour

PERSONAL SAFETY

The traveller does not run any great risks by visiting the Holy Land, despite the scenes of violence sometimes shown on television between Palestinian youths and Israeli troops. Neither Jew nor Arab has any quarrel with visitors to the Holy Land. But it is probably not prudent for travellers in cars with Israeli number plates to visit villages in the West Bank or the Gaza strip — cars in the occupied territories have different number plates. Our route does not visit the occupied territories of the West Bank hill country or the Gaza Strip.

HEALTH

For this region, vaccination is recommended against cholera, typhoid and polio, although no vaccination is required as a condition of entry. In view of the incidence of AIDS, it is probably sensible to take a first-aid pack containing sterile hypodermic needles and other such equipment — available from the London School of Hygiene and Tropical Medicine (tel: 01 631 4408). Visitors should also make certain that their holiday insurance will adequately cover hospital treatment. The visitor is advised to drink bottled water.

DRESS

Jordan is a conservative country so far as women are concerned. Slacks are acceptable, but shorts and bare-back dresses are not. Modest dress is also necessary throughout the Holy Land when visiting churches, mosques and holy places. Comfortable walking shoes are essential for visiting the archaeological sites. The temperature can vary, even in high summer. Temperatures can fluctuate between a hot midday level of around 97°F (36°C) in Jericho to a cool evening of 61°F (16°C) in Jerusalem. Visitors should travel light, but should carry some warm clothes.

ELECTRICITY SUPPLY

The electricity supply both in Jordan and in Israel is 220 A.C. volts, suitable for British equipment. But the visitor is advised to bring an international adaptor to fit any socket.

PHOTOGRAPHY

The light in the Holy Land is particularly good in the spring for photography — later in the year, there is a great deal of dust in the atmosphere creating a hazy effect. There are places, such as the Allenby/Hussein Bridge, where photography is not allowed. Probably the best way of recording your holiday is with a video camera. But electrical equipment of this kind is much more expensive in the Holy Land than in the United Kingdom — you will find that your possession of a video camera will be recorded in your passport and you may be charged a deposit which will be refunded when you leave the country, with the camera still in your possession.

ACCOMMODATION

There are plenty of hotels at Amman, Jerusalem, Tiberias and the coastal resorts of the Holy Land, ranging from modest to very well-appointed. Almost invariably, they offer twin-bedded rooms and charge extra if the traveller wants single accommodation. But outside Amman and Aqaba there is a shortage of hotels in the Kingdom of Jordan. The Forum Hotel at Petra offers good facilities. But at Petra accommodation is also available at a government-run Rest House. The rooms are large, with beds for up to four visitors — not suitable for travellers determined to preserve a degree of privacy. Visitors are not expected to share rooms, however, except when the Rest House is crowded. Rooms should be booked in advance at the Rest House both for individual and group bookings.

CURRENCY
The Jordanian currency is the dinar: 1 Jordanian dinar (1JD) = 100 piastres = 1000 fils. The Israeli currency is the shekel. But the high inflation rates in the State of Israel in recent years has prompted most prices to be quoted in U.S. dollars. The people of the Holy Land in general are adept at working out exchange rates and almost any currency is acceptable.

TELEPHONE AND POSTAGE
Fairly recently, one guide book to Jordan admitted that trying to use the telephone 'can reduce one to tears'. But the telephone system is now much improved, and international calls to Jordan can be made on 010 962. The area codes are as follows: Amman 6; Irbid 2; Zerqa 9; Aqaba 3; Salt 5.

The Israeli telephone system is good. International calls to Israel can be made on 010 972. The area codes are as follows: Akko 4; Afula 6; Ashdod 55; Asqelon 51; Beer Sheva 57; Eilat 59; Hadera 6; Haifa 4; Jerusalem 2; Nazareth 6; Netanya 53; Rehovot 8; Safed 6; Tel Aviv 3; Tiberias 6. Area codes are included with telephone numbers in this book only where it is necessary to avoid confusion. Hotels put large surcharges on calls to the U.K. and it is best to make such calls from a post office.

Post is not delivered in Jordan or in Israel but must be collected from a P.O. Box. Postage out can usually be arranged through reception at the various hotels.

SHOPS AND OFFICES
Trading usually takes place between 8 a.m. and noon and again between 4 p.m. and 7 p.m. It is worth remembering that the Islamic weekly holy day is Friday, the Jewish weekly holy day is Saturday and that the Christian weekly holy day is Sunday. Shops and offices in different parts of the Holy Land will be closed on those days — the effect is particularly striking in Jerusalem.

The Itinerary

How to Use the Itinerary

The Itinerary begins in Amman, Jordan. I suggest you arrive in Amman the evening before you begin following the suggested route. The tour ends in Petra, Jordan, from where you need to book transport in advance to return to Queen Alia Airport. Details of hotels, restaurants, and general information on main tours are found at the end of each day's route. A map of the whole Itinerary is found on p. 8-9, and detailed daily maps are as follows:

Days 1, 2, 3, 9 and 10: pp 68-9.
Days 4-8: pp. 112-13.

For a touring map of Israel I suggest the *Barzak Guide to Israel*, available from most bookshops. The main disadvantage of this map is that the desert road to Petra (Day 9) has been superimposed with plans of Jerusalem. However, a good map of Jordan is supplied by the Jordanian Embassy when visitors apply for a visa.

For an authoritative series of maps illustrating the different historical periods I suggest the *Student Map Manual: Historical Geography of the Bible Lands*, from Pictorial Archives Est., Old School, P.O. Box 19823, Jerusalem.

Map references are given at the beginning of each day for the main places visited (longitude is given first, then latitude, reading from the perimeter of any map using the Israel Grid System).

DAY 1

Amman, Madaba, Mount Nebo, Jerash and Amman: approximately 90 miles

The people of, say, the twelfth century B.C. would describe today's route as an excursion from the capital city of the Ammonites into the mountains of Moab through the Israelite territories of Gad and Reuben — it would, I imagine, have been perilous to attempt it. Spend the morning at Amman before setting off south to Madaba, the 'city of mosaics'. Turn off to visit Mount Nebo, where Moses was granted the sight of the promised land before his death. Then follow the route of the ancient King's Highway north past Hisban to spend the evening at Jerash, the best preserved example of a Roman city in the Middle East, before returning to your hotel in Amman.

Overnight at Amman.

Map references
Amman   240:148
Madaba   226:124
Mount Nebo   220:132
Jerash   234:188

Route shown p. 68.   *The pattern of the Madeba mosaic map*

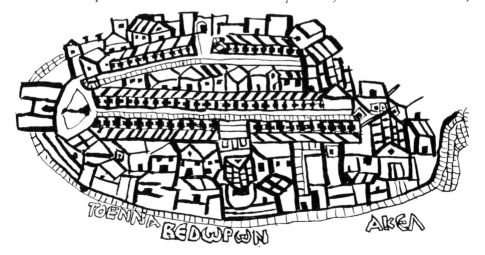

Breakfast in Amman.

Amman

Amman has a population of about 650,000 and is growing rapidly, a maze of modern streets spread over a series of hills. The city illustrates an interesting trait in the Arab mentality. 'Finding your way out of Amman is a nightmare,' said a friend of mine who had hired a car. Instinctively I think, the Arabs create urban labyrinths to escape friend and foe alike. But elegant modern shops, hotels and houses are springing up everywhere, and there is a feeling of great vitality in this city of white stone and wrought iron, green-domed mosques and marble imported from Bethlehem. I asked a taximan why the television aerials are shaped everywhere in imitation of the Eiffel Tower. 'People have much money', he said cryptically, 'and not sense.' This is a new city of the Middle East, built almost entirely in this century. Yet traces of houses dating from about 7000 B.C. have recently been excavated at Ain Ghazal in the suburbs — Amman is a modern city, nine thousand years old.

This was the biblical Rabbah of the Ammonites, where was found the legendary iron bedstead of Og the giant king of Bashan. Three thousand years ago, stories about giants were common — almost certainly, the 'bedstead' was a large, basalt sarcophagus. The Ammonites themselves were an Arab people, originating like many others among the nomadic tribes of the shifting sands of Arabia. In the Old Testament, there was enmity between the Ammonites and the Israelites. It explains perhaps why the Ammonites were reputedly a people of lustful character and irregular habits, and why doubts were cast on their parentage (Genesis 19, 38).

The archaeology shows that Amman first became an important regional capital in the twelfth century B.C. In the following century David, king of Israel, was friendly with Nahash, king of Ammon, and on the death of his friend sent messengers to offer condolences to Hanum his son. But Hanum had the messengers beaten up, thinking they were spies. It led to war. David's army attacked and took the Ammonite capital — events which also played their part in a famous love story. On the king's orders, Uriah the Hittite was placed in the forefront of the battle — to die because David had seduced Uriah's beautiful wife Bathsheeba.

In Hellenistic times, the city was renamed Philadelphia and was then an important centre of trade and Greek culture. The Romans under Pompey the Great took the city in 63 B.C. and included it in the Decapolis — a league of ten transjordanian city states. Philadelphia entered a golden age under the rule of imperial Rome, and the finest archaelological remains to be seen at Amman date from this period. But the Ammonites as a nation pass out of history in Roman times — people still spoke of them in the third century but only as an obscure Arab tribe. Yet Philadelphia continued to grow and expand.

This was a centre of Christianity and the seat of a bishop in the Byzantine era. The city was taken by the forces of Islam in A.D. 635, and was renamed Amman. For reasons unknown, this ancient capital city was abandoned in about A.D. 1300 after the Crusades, and the use of the site was not revived until the nineteenth century when the Ottoman Turks established a village here for Circassian refugees from Russia. In 1922, Amman became the capital of the Emir Abdullah and in 1946 the new Hashemite Kingdom of Jordan was centred on the city.

The main historic features of Amman are close together and can be visited easily. The citadel, called Jebel Qal'ah, hangs 300 ft above the city centre and is surrounded by steep slopes on all sides. It involves a climb up steps to the apex. The visitor will see a great mixture of archaeological remains from different periods at the citadel, but they are dominated by fine Roman buildings. The entrance leads into a spacious court in the centre of which stands the remains of a temple of Hercules built in the second century. But there are also traces at the citadel of buildings and fortifications from many periods. The temple of Hercules, for instance, is built on the site of a sacred rock probably used for sacrifice as early as 3000 B.C. To the north are the remains of a fine Arab palace from the Umayyad period, the headquarters of a large Islamic complex built in the seventh century A.D. The Amman Archaeological Museum is also to be found on the citadel, a small but well-presented collection arranged in chronological order.

To the south below the citadel, the remains of the Roman lower city stand on the banks of the Wadi Amman. The visitor can see the remains of a nymphaeum — a fountain decorated with nymphs. In this area, too, are the remains of a market place, and a fine theatre from the first century A.D. This was the main shopping area of Philadelphia and the centre of civic administration in Roman times. In the eastern vaults of the theatre, well worth

45

a visit, can be found the fascinating Jordan Museum of Popular Traditions and in the western vaults is the Amman Folklore Museum.

The visit to the antiquities of Amman should take about two and a half hours and can be followed by lunch, probably at your overnight hotel.

After lunch leave Amman on the airport road, then turn right towards Madaba about 19 miles to the south. The scenery at this stage is as flat as a board, verging on desert.

Madaba

Nowadays, Madaba is a small, busy market town, rather untidy. It was originally a Moabite city. But around 2200 B.C., the city fell to the Amorites. These were marauding desert tribes from Syria and Arabia which descended in wild razzias (sudden raids) on many of the cities of the Middle East. In time, the Amorites were urbanized and, eight hundred years later, when the Israelites led by Moses arrived east of the Jordan, Madaba was ruled by Sihon, king of the Amorites. Sihon refused the Israelites passage through his lands — it led to a pitched battle and Sihon's defeat. During the Israelite settlement, Madaba was allocated to the tribe of Reuben. But in the ninth century B.C., the city was retaken by Mesha, king of Moab.

The city changed hands again and again. Jews, Nabateans, Romans, Byzantines and Arabs ruled in turn. Finally in A.D. 747, an earthquake destroyed the city and the site was abandoned. For over twelve hundred years, all that remained was a solitary mound adjoining the desert highway. The site was resettled in the nineteenth century by migrants from Kerak, see p. 138-9. As the new settlers dug the foundations of their houses, they were surprised to unearth superb mosaics of Roman and Byzantine origin. Even today there are many mosaics in private houses at Madaba — some are shown to the public for a small fee.

In 1884, a monk from Madaba wrote to the Greek Patriarch of Jerusalem telling him of a mosaic pavement he had found, depicting Jericho, Jerusalem, Gaza and many other places mentioned in the Bible. The letter remained on file for about four years, but eventually a mason was sent to build a church over the mosaic. He destroyed most of it while building the church, then reported that the mosaic was of no great importance. What remains is the famous sixth-century Madaba mosaic map of the Middle East, orientated east/west, based on Roman military maps, made in the Byzantine period, incorporating biblical texts and illustrating the topography of the Bible.

The Greek Orthodox Church of St George at Madaba now houses the mosaic map.

Originally, the map was about 75 feet long by 20 feet wide and depicted many places, including Madaba itself. But what remains is certainly worth seeing. Notice too the fine pictures in the church, in particular an ancient icon showing the baptism of Jesus — remember the River Jordan where it happened is only 30 miles away.

But Madaba was a great centre of mosaics long before the making of the biblical map in the Byzantine period. The Madaba Museum also contains mosaics from the Roman period, notably a large pavement depicting Achilles carrying a lyre, accompanied by Patroclus and by Persis, his favourite slave girl. The museum also contains traditional costumes, jewellery and carpets from the Madaba region. Carpet making — a craft similar in many ways to mosaic making — is a family tradition, passed on from father to son. In workshops in the side-streets near the Church of St George, the visitor can see the carpet makers working on ancient looms, and Madaba carpets are on sale in the shops around the church.

Leave Madaba and take the route northwest (6 miles) to Mount Nebo and follow the signs to Siyagha.

Mount Nebo

Mount Nebo is the highest peak of a mountainous region overlooking the northern end of the Dead Sea. The hill of Siyagha on the west side of Mount Nebo is traditionally believed to be the vantage point from which Moses viewed the promised land before his death. In about A.D. 390, a nun called Egeria visited the region — her diary was rediscovered in a library in Italy in 1884. She tells of Byzantine monks living in the vicinity of Mount Nebo. The hilltop at Siyagha had been abandoned for well over a thousand years when, inspired by Egeria's diary, the work of excavating the site was begun by the Franciscans in 1933. Egeria had found a tiny trefoil church which had been converted by the monks from a mausoleum built in the Roman period. The

47

excavators found the walls of a much larger sixth-century Byzantine church, divided into three aisles — the remains of the building of Egeria's time were found in the sanctuary area. Around this church were monastic cells, kitchens and dormitories.

On arriving at Siyagha, look first at the valley spread below. The countryside falling away into the rift is an untidy bedspread of desert punctured with winding wadis and patches of cultivation. On a clear day the spires of the churches of Jerusalem are visible, and to the right is the rich oasis of Jericho. The Italian sculptor Giovanni Fantoni made the bronze serpent on a pole overlooking this scene — reminding the visitor that Moses raised a fiery serpent in the wilderness to cure the Israelites who had been poisoned by serpents (Numbers 21, 8).

The long low church at Siyagha, dedicated to Moses, has been built to incorporate the remains of the Byzantine church. Inside are mosaics, dating from the fourth, fifth and sixth centuries. Particularly impressive is the perfectly preserved mosaic in the north aisle, dated A.D. 541, depicting hunting and pastoral scenes. We are told in an inscription that the makers of this mosaic were Soelos, Kaiomos and Elias. Other mosaics in the church depict bulls, deer, peacocks and crows. And there are many inscriptions in Greek giving the names of donors and mosaic makers. A simple mosaic cross from the fourth century, still to be seen in the church, adorned the sanctuary which Egeria saw.

Detour

To the south of Mount Nebo is the site of the biblical city called Nebo — now called El Mekhayyat. The road to the tel leads off to the right on the way back from Siyagha to Madaba. The Franciscans began excavations at the tel in 1935, and the remains of five Byzantine churches have been found.A fine mosaic depicting hunting and harvesting scenes can be seen in the remains of the church of St George, dedicated in A.D. 536. And exceptionally fine mosaics of pastoral scenes can be found at the church of Saints Lot and Procopius. The earliest church, in the Wadi Afrit below the tel, is dedicated to Saints Amos and Caiseos. Here in the Chapel of Priest John, added to the church in the latter half of the sixth century, the central figure in a rich mosaic is the personification of Mother Earth crowned with fruits and grain. Beyond the Wadi Afrit the Moabite hills extend south, an undulating desert scene.

The visit to Madaba and Siyagha should take about three hours — longer if it includes the detour. Afterwards, take the road north following the ancient King's Highway to Na'ur. As with the road from Amman to Madaba, you are passing through the flat, unrelieved landscape of the transjordanian plateau.

Hisban

Notice the modern village called Hisban, about five miles along the King's Highway from Madaba. Tel Hesban which rises north of the village is the site of the biblical Heshbon, a city of the tribe of Gad during the period of the Israelite settlement. But the remains of most of the buildings on the tel date from Roman times — of particular interest is a large subterranean cave which was used as an artisan's workshop. The archaeologists have also found walls from the twelfth and eleventh centuries B.C. and pieces of pottery and ostraca — inscriptions on unglazed pottery — from the sixth century B.C.

Continue north along the modern road to Jerash via Na'ur.

Jerash

To a large extent Jerash is a vast Roman archaeological site, although part of it is taken up with a small village. The remains of colonnaded streets and buildings extend in all directions.

The city was first built in the Hellenistic period by Perdiccas, one of the generals of Alexander the Great. For centuries, this was an important link in a string of fortified cities to keep marauding desert tribes out of the Jordan valley. The city was taken by the Romans during the campaign of Pompey the Great in 63 B.C. Afterwards, Jerash — called Gerasa, the original version of the name — was a busy centre of trade, one of the league of the ten transjordanian cities of the Decapolis. Nearly two thousand years later the site is dominated by elegant Roman columns, the streets laid out by the Roman town planners. The marks of chariot wheels can still be seen in the paved roadways of the market street.

The heyday of Jerash was the third century A.D., when trade had brought great prosperity to this cosmopolitan city of temples, theatres and gymnasia, the colonnaded streets punctuated with fountains and monuments. There were further developments in the Byzantine era when magnificent churches were built, ornamented with fine mosaics. Jerash fell into Islamic hands in A.D. 635. Earthquakes destroyed much of the city in the ninth century. Finally, the Crusaders destroyed the walls of Jerash in A.D. 1122, and the site was abandoned. The city was rediscovered in 1806 by the German explorer Ulrich Jasper Seetzen.

Approaching Jerash from the south, the remains of a triumphal arch, built in A.D. 130. to honour a visit by the Emperor Hadrian, can be seen about five hundred yards south of the city. Nearby are the remains of the hippodrome — a Roman chariot racetrack. The track was about 350 yards long, and at the south end are the compartments from which the racing chariots started. On the southern hill, just inside the remains of the city walls, is the temple of Zeus, originally built in the first century. A Roman theatre which held about 3000 spectators stands nearby — notice that some of the seats are numbered.

The remains of the city centre are approached through a remarkable oval piazza which leads into a cardo — a long market street lined with elegant Corinthian columns. Little else remains now, but in Roman times this street was built up on both sides with shops filled with the goods which flowed in vast quantities along the trade routes of the Middle East — pottery from the Aegean, silks from far-away India, spices from Arabia. Jerash was an excellent shopping and trading centre in the Roman era. Two small piazzas mark the intersections of this market street with the other main streets of the city. To the left of the cardo, behind an elaborate nymphaeum, can be seen the remains of the Byzantine cathedral, approached from the street by a monumental colonnade. Built in about A.D. 365 over a Roman temple, it was probably the earliest Christian church at Jerash. To the north stand the remains of the Temple of Artemis, built about A.D. 150. The approach to this magnificent temple is from the east, across a bridge over the Wadi Jerash leading to gateways, colonnades, courtyards and staircases. The remains of the temple itself, at the apex of a high podium, now dominate the scene.

There are many other Roman and Byzantine remains at Jerash. The three Byzantine churches to the west of the Temple of Artemis, all built around 530 A.D., contain the finest mosaics to be found in the city. The Roman road going north out of Jerash led to another city of the Decapolis called Pella — good roads linked these city states. Just over half a mile to the north can be found the Festival Theatre of ancient Gerasa, overlooking a pool. Every three years, the festival of Maiumas in honour of Artemis was celebrated here with drama and water sports. Twice in the fourth century, these festivities were prohibited because they included nude shows and promiscuity. Nowadays, in much more decorous festivities, artists and craftsmen from the Arab world and beyond take part in the Jerash Festival of Culture and Arts which is held annually during August.

Dinner at Jerash

A meal can be taken at the Rest House at Jerash. If these travels are taking place in the period between May and October, a fitting end to Day 1 would be to attend the 'son et lumière' performance which is held at dusk each evening at Jerash. The commentary on the ancient history of the city is given in English, French, German or Arabic.

Day 1 is completed with a return to the hotel at Amman.

Museums

The Amman Archaeological Museum (tel: 638795) on the citadel and the Amman Folklore Museum (tel: 637196) in the east wing of the Roman theatre are open every day except on Tuesdays. The Jordan Museum of Popular Traditions (tel: 622316) in the west wing of the theatre is open daily. The Madaba Museum is open daily except on Tuesdays.

The Jerash Rest House
Postage to: P.O. Box 2863 Amman
Tel: 04451146

A Selection of Amman Hotels

Amman Marriott, five star, Omar Ben Abu Rabah Street, Shmeisani, P.O. Box 926333 (tel: 660100)

Regency Palace, five star, Queen Alia Street, Sports City Road, P.O. Box 927000 (tel: 660000)

Holiday Inn, five star, Al Hussein Ben Ali Street, Jabal Amman, P.O. Box 6399 (tel: 663100)

Jordan Intercontinental, five star, Queen Zein Street, Jebel Amman, P.O. Box 35014 (tel: 641361)

Amra Hotel, superior four star, Sixth Circle, Wadi Al Seer, P.O. Box 950555 (tel: 815071)

Middle East, four star, Arab College Street, Shmeinasi, P.O. Box 19224 (tel: 667150)

Ambassador, four star, Abdul Hamid Sharaf Street, Shmeisani, P.O. Box 925390 (tel: 665161)

Grand Palace, four star, Queen Alia Street, Jabal Al Hussein, P.O. Box 6916 (tel: 661121)

San Rock, four star, Um Uthaina, Jabal Amman, P.O. Box 9032 (tel: 813800)

Canary, three star, Jabal Weibdeh, P.O. Box 9062 (tel: 638353)

Caravan, three star, Police Academy Street, Jabal Weibdeh, P.O. Box 9062 (tel: 661195)

Please note: Many streets in Amman have at least two names — the official designation and the name by which it is generally known. Sharia Al-Malikah Alia, for instance, is also called Queen Alia Street, Sports City Road, University Road or Suweileh Road. It adds in no small degree to the confusion of this urban labyrinth. It explains why guides are expected to pass an examination.

Tour Operator

The Guiding Star office in Amman is in Prince Mohammad Street, P.O. Box 2766 (tel: 642526).

Restaurants in Amman

Jabri, King Hussein Street (tel: 624108) — Jordanian specialities at reasonable prices.

Jordan Restaurant, Post Office Square (tel: 638333) is run by the same family as runs the **Jabri**, and has a take-away.

Jerusalem Restaurant — also known as Al Quds, King Hussein Street (tel: 630168) — Middle East cuisine at reasonable prices.

Taxis

Amra Taxi Office, Amra Hotel, Wadi al Seer, Sixth Circle, P.O. Box 7601 (tel: 815071)

AMMAN: USEFUL INFORMATION

Ministry of Tourism and Antiquities, Zahran Street, Jabal Amman, P.O. Box 224 (tel: 643211)

Population:	65,000
Altitude:	2,600 ft
Facilities:	hotels — five to three star, restaurants, museums and archaeological sites

Allenby/Hussein Bridge 26 miles

The Temple Platform with the Dome of the Rock

DAY 2

Amman, the River Jordan, Jerusalem: approximately 55 miles

Leave Amman early to be in Jerusalem by midday. Cross the Jordan at Jericho, the most famous river crossing in the world. Nine thousand years ago migrants forded the river here and destroyed Jericho with great violence, the earliest known use of this crossing — to be followed over the millennia by a myriad other warring armies, migrants and travellers. Jesus of Nazareth himself crossed the Jordan here. After leaving the bridge, pass through the rich oasis of Jericho to the desert road which rises to Jerusalem in the hills. No journey could be more evocative than this. Spend the remainder of the day and overnight in Jerusalem.

Map reference
Jerusalem 172:131

Route shown p. 68.

Early breakfast in Amman.

Crossing the King Hussein/Allenby Bridge

Leave by coach or taxi at about 6.30 a.m. — the bridge is open only during the morning each day. Remember that papers are required from the Ministry of Tourism at Amman in order to be allowed to cross the bridge. The road runs west from Amman on the transjordanian plateau then snakes down into the open plain at the base of the rift valley, over twelve hundred feet below sea level.

Passports are inspected at the Jordanian checkpoint before travellers can embark on a bus which runs a shuttle service across the bridge — no photographs allowed. The crossing is made on the shuttle bus or on a tour operator's bus — private cars are not allowed across the bridge. Poets have dreamed of this crossing:

> Sweet fields beyond the swelling flood
> Stand dressed in living green;
> So to the Jews old Canaan stood,
> While Jordan rolled between.

It's just as well Isaac Watts never saw it — this is a landscape of the moon, unbelievably barren. Over thousands of years, the torrential winter floods have fashioned and terraced the grey marl of the base of the valley into a myriad castellated shapes. The river itself cannot be seen — it has dug its own grave and runs in a deep ditch. Every morning a traffic jam of heavy lorries builds up on the other side, laden with cargoes to be taken into Jordan — bananas, oranges and grapefruit from the Jericho oasis, or great slabs of white Bethlehem marble. The occasional lorry escapes and comes over as the shuttle bus approaches the bridge.

The crossing itself involves a short bumpy ride over a metal-framed wooden bridge which hangs over a dank stream overgrown with tamarisk and tangled bush. In ancient times, this was the jungle called the 'pride of Jordan' — there were lions here in the Middle Ages. But so much water has been taken for irrigation that the river is reduced to very little. Suddenly submachine guns peer out from a hilltop where an Israeli flag is planted; the bus trundles over to the long low buildings of the checkpoint. Most of the Israeli troops are young conscripts who look as though they ought to be at college — only occasionally is a guard arrogant or bad tempered. Suitcases are piled on trolleys and taken away. Travellers disembark and queue for attention.

This is no great international transit complete with restaurants, tills ringing in duty-free shops. It's like coming in at somebody's back door — also, it seems, the hottest place on earth. The Israelis don't stamp your passport — travellers with passports stamped by Israel will not be admitted back into Jordan. For some reason, apples and bottles of water are not allowed across the frontier — some people drink and munch their way through the customs. A bridge tax must be paid. The Israeli supervision of travellers extends well beyond the frontier. 'How are you getting to Jerusalem?' a young soldier asks. Taxis and buses are drawn up outside.

You may notice on your maps of the area the Abdullah Bridge further south, this is not available for crossing into Israel.

The road from the bridge leads into Jericho, an Arab town of palms and orchards. Route 90, the modern road through the town, runs south in the direction of the Dead Sea. About three miles outside Jericho, Route 1 to the right is the modern road which runs through the desert rising towards Jerusalem in the hills. (The ancient road from Jerusalem to Jericho, made famous in Jesus' parable of the Good Samaritan, will be visited on Day 3.) It is not possible to predict how long the entry formalities at the border are likely to take, but an early start should mean that travellers can lunch at their Jerusalem hotel.

Jerusalem will be used as a base for part of this itinerary — so there will be ample opportunity to come to know this remarkable city. I recommend you spend the afternoon visiting the Old City.

Jerusalem the golden

Before 1967, the international border between the Hashemite Kingdom of Jordan and the State of Israel ran through Jerusalem itself. The barbed wire, the sentries and the frontier posts disappeared when the Israelis took East Jerusalem in the Six Day War — traces of bullets can still be seen scored in the grey walls of Notre Dame north of the Old City. What was the no man's land is now a park, made green by the eternal application of sprinklers. Yet this city is still divided. Jerusalem East or West, each is wrapped in a distinctive culture and tradition. Very few buses run between them. The modern streets of West Jerusalem are elegant, lined with shops and hotels which would look at home in Paris, Berlin or New York. Only the orthodox with their black homburgs and ringlets are a visible reminder of Zionism. The streets of East Jerusalem, on the other hand, are thronged with scrabbling children, be-cassocked antique Muslims, pretty, painted Arab girls, old women selling prickly pears and shops vending chickpeas. West Jerusalem is occidental Jerusalem, but East Jerusalem is nothing if not oriental.

But whether one stays east or west, the Old City is the magnet which draws the traveller. Begin at the Jaffa Gate, one of the few places where modern traffic can enter the Old City — a section of the ancient city wall has been demolished to let in the cars. But enter through the massive archway of the old gate itself. It involves a right-angled turn — because when sentries marched the city walls, no gate allowed an enemy to charge straight in. To the right is the citadel, nowadays a museum and exhibition centre. It's certainly worth a visit, but not immediately. Instead, plunge out of the brightness of the street into the confusing, dazzling world of the souk.

This is a kaleidoscope of assorted peoples, black African, yellow Oriental or pallid European, enticed into the shops by plump Arab traders: 'Welcome, welcome! You Eeenglish? You spik to me . . . you buy . . . you buy.' Crusader arches, trailing telephone wires and Turkish wrought-iron window baskets hang overhead. Tangs of leather, spices, bad drains, fresh pitta bread and ground coffee bid for attention. Carts laden with Coca Cola or olivewood camels are shunted up the donkey steps. The place is a gigantic tourist trap — you must argue to survive: 'Twenty-five dollars, cheap . . . you wish to pay in drachmas?' Little men appear out of side alleys. 'Let me show you the Via Dolorosa, sir — the way to Calvary. I insist — you must have official guide! Come this way, sir!' Resist them firmly — or they will whizz you through the souk into the sterile streets beyond, peopled by hymn-singing, twiceborn Americans or grim Franciscans leading columns of French nuns. Buy, instead, a drink of fresh orange — the vendors simply cut the fruit in half and squeeze out the cool juice for you. And examine some of the lovely Arabic silverware on sale in the souk. Such artifacts were sold in the bazaars of Jerusalem in Canaanite, Babylonian, Persian and Roman times. No more venerable or ancient a tradition of trade can be found anywhere. Yet this is not Jerusalem the golden simply because it always was a centre of trade. Where the sunlight glints on the stones, the Old City itself is a mellow gold.

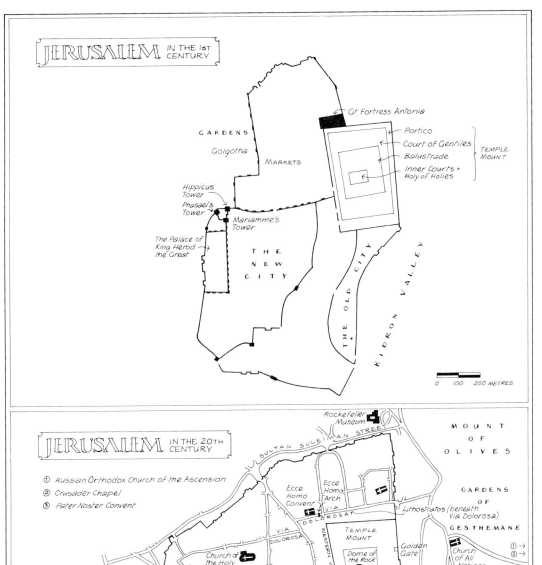

JERUSALEM IN THE 1st CENTURY

Gt Fortress Antonia

GARDENS

Golgotha

MARKETS

Portico
Court of Gentiles
Balustrade
Inner Courts +
Holy of Holies

TEMPLE MOUNT

Hippicus Tower
Phasael's Tower
Mariamme's Tower

The Palace of King Herod the Great

THE NEW CITY

THE OLD CITY

KIDRON VALLEY

0   100   200 METRES

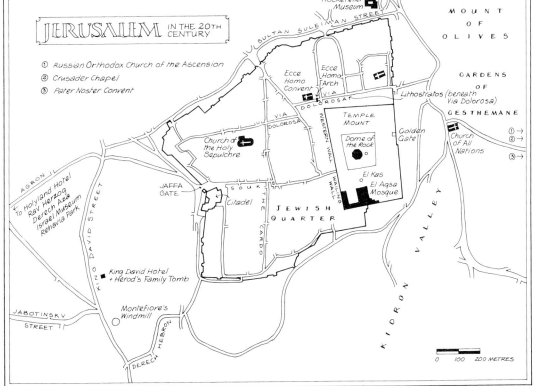

JERUSALEM IN THE 20th CENTURY

① Russian Orthodox Church of the Ascension
② Crusader Chapel
③ Pater Noster Convent

Rockefeller Museum

SULTAN SULEIMAN STREET

MOUNT OF OLIVES

Ecce Homo Convent
Ecce Homo Arch

VIA DOLOROSA

GARDENS OF

Lithostratos (beneath Via Dolorosa)

GESTHEMANE

VIA DOLOROSA

WESTERN WALL

TEMPLE MOUNT

Dome of the Rock

Golden Gate

Church of All Nations

① →
② →
③ →

Church of the Holy Sepulchre

AGRON

To Holyland Hotel
Rav Herzog
Derech Aza
Israel Museum
Rehavia Park

JAFFA GATE

Citadel

SOUK THE CARDO

WAILING WALL

El Kas
El Aqsa Mosque

JEWISH QUARTER

KING DAVID STREET

King David Hotel + Herod's Family Tomb

KIDRON VALLEY

Montefiore's Windmill

JABOTINSKY STREET

DERECH HEBRON

0   100   200 METRES

The history of the Old City

But this is not the Jerusalem of the Bible. After the Israelites arrived in the Holy Land, the tribes established their territories to the north and to the south of Jerusalem. But they did not take this isolated city inhabited by the Jebusites, built on a high narrow ridge surrounded by deep ravines and precipitous mountain slopes.

The city was well nigh impregnable. Defensive walls had been built on the sides of the ridge, and even the problems posed by the water supply had been overcome. The only water supply to Jebusite Jerusalem was the little stream called the Gihon in the deep Valley of the Kidron east of the city. Incredibly, the Jebusites had used the primitive tools of the period to cut a shaft through the solid rock of the ridge down to the stream eighty feet below. Water could be hauled up through the shaft into the city in leather buckets — it added to the difficulties of taking Jerusalem, because there was no need for the defenders to go outside the walls to collect water.

According to the Old Testament, King David took Jerusalem in about 1000 B.C. by sending his men up the water shaft. Strategically, it was brilliant. Afterwards, David was able to unite the Israelite tribes in a common allegiance to his new royal capital, independent of the tribal territories both north and south. Later when there was a plague in the city, David bought the threshing floor of Araunah the Jebusite on the apex of the ridge above Jerusalem. There he built an altar to the God of Israel — he believed it would propitiate the deity and bring the plague to an end. In the following reign, King Solomon built the Temple of the Lord on the site of the threshing floor.

In such a way did Jerusalem become the holy city of Israel.

But Solomon's Temple was destroyed in 587 B.C. by the forces of Nebuchadnezzar II, King of Babylon. The Temple was rebuilt about fifty years later but, so the Old Testament writers said, to such poor standards as to make the loss of the original even more poignant. Two names stand out in the history of Israel when it comes to massive building schemes — Solomon in the tenth century B.C. and King Herod the Great in the first. (The remains of Herod's magnificent palace-fortress at Masada will be visited on Day 3.) When Herod began the task of rebuilding the Temple in Jerusalem in about 20 B.C., his plan vied with the pyramids in grandeur and aimed to supercede the magnificence of Solomon's Temple. The work was still in progress over sixty years after his death. The Temple was nearly a thousand years old during the lifetime of Jesus of Nazareth, but the buildings were in new condition.

Herod began with a major work in civil engineering. A massive earth-moving operation largely filled in the Tyropoeon Valley to the west of the city, and as a base for the new Temple huge retaining walls were built to completely enclose the apex of the ridge in a gigantic platform.

Sadly this magnificent temple complex, the most grandiose of all King Herod's building schemes, lasted only seven years. In A.D. 70, the Temple was entirely destroyed by the Roman army, an act of revenge after the legions had finally quelled the first Jewish revolt against the power of Rome. The Temple at Jerusalem had come to an end, never again to be rebuilt.

Yet this was not the end of the Jewish struggles against imperial Rome. A second Jewish revolt was led by Simon Bar Cochbar in A.D. 132-135. Like the first, it was overthrown. It led to the complete destruction of Jerusalem itself. In place of biblical Jerusalem, a new Roman city called Aelia Capitolina was built. Jews were forbidden the new city and its environs. The Old City of today has seen many changes since Roman times, but it remains the work of the Roman town planners.

The holy city of Jerusalem

The history of the Old City explains the present. Take a street to the right out of the souk and enter the Jewish Quarter. The narrow streets are quieter here, the shops much more elegant — many of them very expensive. Fashionable restaurants and little art galleries abound. In contrast to the souk the Jewish Quarter is a smart neighbourhood in the Old City, but it is rooted in history nevertheless. Here and there, the remains of the Cardo — the original Roman market street — can be seen, flanked with slender columns and Byzantine lock-up shops. This is the long street marked in the Madaba mosaic map (see p. 46-7) — a copy of the Jerusalem part of the map is displayed in one of the streets nearby. Over the centuries Jews have stayed here to pray and study, and there are many schools of Jewish theology in this part of the Old City. Turn left in the Jewish Quarter and wander through the streets until you overlook the great platform, the remains of King Herod the Great's Temple.

But this is now the third holiest shrine in Islam — only Mecca and Medina take precedence. According to the teachings of Islam, the prophet Muhammad in the seventh century was transported from this place to heaven to receive the Holy Qur'an. The golden Dome of the Rock, built about sixty years after the prophet's death, stands where the Altar of Sacrifice of the Jewish Temple once stood. And at the southernmost end of the platform is the silver-domed El Aqsa Mosque built in the eighth century.

Descend from the Jewish Quarter to the pavement which faces the Temple platform. At the entrance, guards will inspect any bags you are carrying — visitors are asked to wear modest dress and to treat the holy places with respect. Jewish men and women are saying their prayers at the 'western wall' of the platform, because it is a surviving part of the Temple of old. It is sometimes called the 'Wailing Wall'. They stand or sit, some of them rocking rhythmically. Prayers and petitions are written on pieces of paper and stuffed into cracks in the ancient wall. The belief is that the links with the world of the Old Testament are stronger here than anywhere else on earth.

But move up onto the platform itself — visitors are welcome except on holy days. Islamic guards stand at the gate, and the rules about modesty of dress are also important here. The El Aqsa Mosque has been rebuilt many times — some of the earlier wood panelling from this building can be seen at the Rockerfeller Museum. To the left, a broad flight of steps will bring you to the upper platform and the Dome of the Rock. Notice the elegant Mameluk arches and the round fountain, called El Kas, used by the faithful to wash themselves in preparation for prayer.

The appearance of the Dome of the Rock has hardly changed over thirteen hundred years of history. This is not a mosque, but a shrine built to protect the sacred rock which was the threshing floor of Araunah the Jebusite and on which King David built the altar of the Lord. This magnificent building is the oldest completely preserved relic of early Islam — a blend of imperial styles, Byzantine and Sassanid. The lower parts of the exterior are panelled with marble while the upper parts are covered in blue tiles, the work of Armenian craftsmen. The golden dome itself was re-covered in gilded aluminium in 1966. Despite many repairs over the centuries, much of the mosaic ornamentation of the interior remains as it was when the shrine was first built. Visitors can obtain permission from the guards to enter the building. See the sacred rock, surrounded on all sides by unique Islamic art.

But an act of imagination can also conjure up the magnificent new Temple which was built here two thousand years ago by King Herod the Great. After visiting the Dome of the Rock, continue in the direction of the northwest corner of the platform where an Islamic college stands high on an L-shaped rock. To protect the Temple, Herod built the great fortress called the Antonia on this rock. Four massive towers, linked by crenellated curtain walls, dominated this corner of the platform. But soon after Herod's death, the administration of Judea and Samaria was placed in the hands of a succession of Roman prefects — Pontius Pilate was appointed A.D. 26. When Jesus overthrew the tables of the moneychangers at the Temple, a Roman garrison manned the Antonia and Roman sentries marched the roof of the covered way which ran from the fortress around the perimeter of the Temple precinct.

The outer court of the Temple was called the Court of the Gentiles — a vast paved area open to all comers. To benefit the treasury, moneychangers at the various gates issued special temple money at a pernicious rate of exchange. Notices warning Gentiles not to enter on pain of death were placed on the balustrade which ran around the inner courts of the Temple — more or less the limits of the upper platform today. Within were a series of walled courts, each exclusive to its members. The Court of Women was a Jewish family court. Within lay the Court of the Men of Israel and the Court of the Priests which encompassed the great bronze Altar of Sacrifice. The Temple itself was a small exquisite building which faced the Altar of Sacrifice and which contained the Holy of Holies, the throne room of the God of Israel himself. One difference between the religion of Israel and other religions of the Middle East was that the God of Israel was not represented by a 'graven image'. The Holy of Holies was therefore an empty room. As the psalmist sang:

The Lord's seat is in heaven: the Lord is in his holy Temple.

The High Priest was allowed to enter the Holy of Holies once a year to offer incense.

Leave the Temple platform by the gate in the northwest corner and join the Via Dolorosa near the Ecce Homo Arch. The belief that this 'Way of Sorrows' follows the footsteps of Jesus on his way to Calvary is based on the idea that he was tried before Pontius Pilate at the Antonia fortress. But it is much more likely that Jesus' trial before the Roman prefect took place at Pilate's headquarters in Jerusalem, a palace built a few decades earlier by King Herod the Great as his royal residence. Nor is it correct to say that the Lithostratos, the pavement beneath the Ecce Homo Convent, was part of the Antonia fortress. This pavement and the Ecco Homo Arch are remains from Aelia Capitolina, the new Roman city built over a century after the crucifixion — notice the game boards scratched into the pavement of the Lithostratos. Yet it is not sufficient to condemn the Via Dolorosa as spurious. Year in, year out, many thousands of pilgrims follow the Via Dolorosa through the streets of the Old City, reliving the events of Jesus' journey to Calvary. It is remarkable and moving, a life-size version of the Stations of the Cross.

Follow the Via Dolorosa until it leads to the Church of the Holy Sepulchre. Jesus did not carry his cross this way, but the site of the great church is not an unlikely place for the crucifixion and the burial of Jesus. It stands within the walls of the Old City today, but was outside biblical Jerusalem. A temple of Aphrodite stood here in Aelia Capitolina. But on the accession of Constantine in the fourth century, the site was cleared and a rock tomb was discovered beneath the building. The remains of a quarry can still be seen in the basement of the church, and there were gardens in this vicinity in the first century. The great untidy building conveys nothing of the atmosphere of Golgotha, the 'place of the skull' where Jesus was crucified, nor yet of the garden of spring flowers of the first Easter. Yet it is very likely that this was indeed the place.

The Old City of Jerusalem is a perennial source of fascination for visitors, its mysteries not to be resolved in an afternoon. Work your way from the Church of the Holy Sepulchre back to the Jaffa Gate. If there is time, visit the citadel. No greater mixture of styles and periods can be seen anywhere. Notice the large tower with embossed stonework at its base to the left of the entrance to the exhibition centre. This is what remains of Phasael, one of three towers built by King Herod the Great to protect his royal residence in Jerusalem. Apart from this tower, nothing remains of Herod's palace. But somewhere in this vicinity, Jesus of Nazareth was brought before Pilate to be condemned to death in the presence of a large crowd.

Lunch and overnight in Jerusalem.

The Exhibition Centre at the Citadel
Open daily 8.30 a.m.-4.30 p.m., except Friday when it is open until 2 p.m.
Multi-screen audio-visual presentation about Jerusalem 8.30 and 10.30 a.m.,
12.30, 2.30 and 6 p.m. (Morning showings only on Fridays, no showings on
Saturdays.)

A Selection of Jerusalem Hotels
King David, five star, 23 King David Street, West Jerusalem (tel: 221111)
This is probably the most famous hotel in the Middle East, on a hill in West
Jerusalem overlooking the Old City. The King David was used as the main
British administrative headquarters during the mandate — a wing was blown
up as Jewish activists encouraged the British to withdraw from Palestine.

Jerusalem Hilton, five star, Givat Ram (tel: 536151), West Jerusalem
— a high rise hotel overlooking the modern city.

Inter Continental Hotel, five star, Mount of Olives, East Jerusalem
(tel: 282551)

Sonesta Hotel, four star, 2 Wolfson Street, Givat Ram, West Jerusalem
(tel: 528221)

Holyland, four star, Harav Uziel Street, Bayit Vegan, West Jerusalem
(tel: 630261). In the grounds of this hotel on the outskirts of West Jerusalem is
a model of the City at the outbreak of the Jewish revolt in A.D. 66 — to be
visited on Day 8 of these travels.

American Colony, four star, Nablus Road, East Jerusalem, (tel: 242421)
It was founded by American philanthropists in the nineteenth century, but is
now one of the best hotels in East Jerusalem — features in John Le Carre's
novel *The Little Drummer Girl*.

St George, four star, East Jerusalem, P.O. Box 19548 (tel: 282571)

Jerusalem Tower, four star, 32 Hillel Street, West Jerusalem (tel: 222161)

Mount Scopus, three star, Sheikh Jarrah, East Jerusalem (tel: 284891)

Strand, three star, 4 Ibn Jubeir Street, East Jerusalem (tel: 280279)

Ram Hotel, three star, 342 Jaffa Road, West Jerusalem (tel: 535231)

Hospices
Notre Dame of Jerusalem, four star standard, Damascus Road, East Jerusalem, P.O. Box 20531 (tel: 289723)

A Selection of Restaurants
The **Philadelphia**, Al-Zahara Street, East Jerusalem (tel: 289770) is renowned for Middle East cooking. But go hungry — the food comes in waves.

El Marrakesh, 4 King David Street, West Jerusalem (tel: 227577) for French and Moroccan cooking — there is a floor show here three nights a week.

Backstage, 20 Marcus Street, West Jerusalem (tel: 669351) — fish a speciality.

In West Jerusalem, there are innumerable excellent little courtyard eating places in Ben Yehuda Street and the surrounding side streets.

Car Hire
Avis, 22 King David Street (tel: 249001)
Hertz, 18 King David Street (tel: 231351)
Europcar, 8 King David Street (tel: 248464)

JERUSALEM: USEFUL INFORMATION
Israeli Government Tourist Information Office: 24 King George Street, West Jerusalem (tel: 241281)

Population:	360,000
Altitude:	1,989-2,711 ft
Facilities:	hotels — five to three star, restaurants, museums and archaeological sites

Tel Aviv 39 miles, Tiberias 98 miles

DAY 3

Jerusalem, Jericho, Qumran, Ein Gedi, Masada, Jerusalem: approximately 123 miles

Today's route encompasses a round trip leaving Jerusalem early in the morning to visit Jericho. See the tel of perhaps the most ancient city in the world — people lived at the oasis over ten thousand years ago. See the remains of sumptuous palaces built to take advantage of the wonderful climate at Jericho. Herod the Great's winter palace was built in the Wadi Qilt: and to the north are the ruins of Hisham's Palace, in the seventh century a magnificent centre of Islamic culture and art. Then travel south along the shores of the Dead Sea to have lunch by the remains of the monastery at Qumran, where the Dead Sea Scrolls were found in 1947. Bathe in the Dead Sea at Ein Gedi, then travel south to Masada, the desert fortress built by King Herod the Great and used by the Jewish zealots as their final retreat in their struggles against imperial Rome. Return to Jerusalem.

Map references

Jericho	193:140
Qumran	193:127
Ein Gedi	187:096
Masada	183:080

Route shown p. 68.

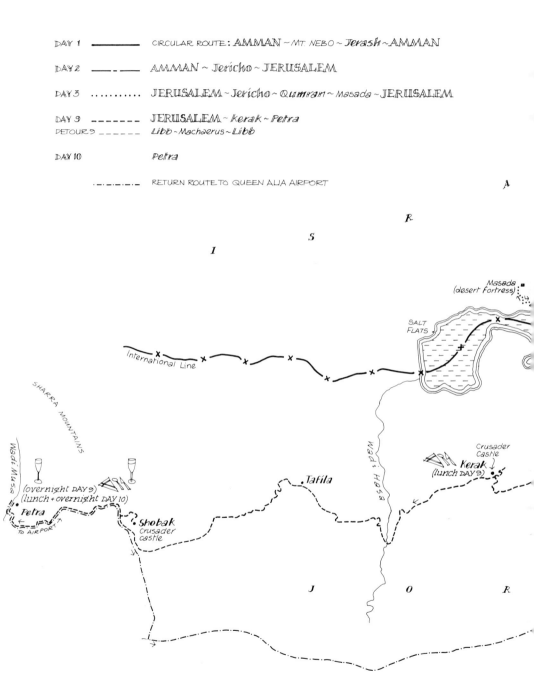

DAY 1 ———— CIRCULAR ROUTE : AMMAN ~ MT. NEBO ~ Jerash ~ AMMAN

DAY 2 —·—·— AMMAN ~ Jericho ~ JERUSALEM

DAY 3 ·········· JERUSALEM ~ Jericho ~ Qumran ~ Masada ~ JERUSALEM

DAY 9 ——————— JERUSALEM ~ kerak ~ Petra
DETOUR 9 —————— Libb ~ Machaerus ~ Libb

DAY 10 Petra

·—··—··—· RETURN ROUTE TO QUEEN ALIA AIRPORT

A

R

S

I

Masada
(desert fortress)

SALT
FLATS

International Line

SHARRA MOUNTAINS

Wadi Musa

(overnight DAY 9)
(lunch + overnight DAY 10)

Petra

TO AIRPORT

Shobak
crusader
castle

Tafila

Wadi Hasa

Crusader
Castle

Kerak
(lunch DAY 9)

J   O   R

DAY
1·2·3·9·10

N

L

E

JERUSALEM
(lunch + overnight
DAY 2 + 8)
(overnight DAY 3)

Wadi Qilt

Inn of
the Good
Samaritan

Monastery of
St George of Choziba
Herod the Great's winter palace

Monastery
Qumran
(lunch DAY 3)

Hisham's Palace
The Tel
Jericho

RIVER JORDAN

Ein Gedi

D   e   a   d   S   e   a

Allenby/King Hussain Bridge

Wadi Mujib

Machaerus
(Palace Fortress
of Herod the
Great)

MT. NEBO

Siyagha

Mekhayyat

Hisban

Jerash

detour

Libb

KINGS HIGHWAY   Na'ur

Madaba

AMMAN (lunch + overnight
DAY 1)

D   A   N

Queen Alia
Airport

Breakfast in Jerusalem.

Begin by collecting a car or a minibus in Jerusalem, I suggest from one of the international car-hire companies in King David Street — to be rented for six days. Then follow Route 1 east of Jerusalem. About nine miles along the modern highway stands the Inn of the Good Samaritan. Usually, a bedouin tent is set up nearby for tourists to visit. There is a fire inside the tent tended by the owner, and around him the metal cups and jugs used when making sweet strong bedouin coffee, seasoned with sesame seeds. After leaving the Inn of the Good Samaritan, take the narrow road to the left signposted to the Wadi Qilt. This is the road 'from Jerusalem to Jericho' made famous in the parable of the Good Samaritan, where a traveller was set upon by robbers. In the first century, this was a Roman road maintained by the legionaries who charged the travellers a toll.

About two miles along this ancient road is the spectacular Greek Orthodox monastery of St George of Choziba, plastered along the face of the cliffs. A mountain path will take you down to the monastery and the caves beyond, well worth a visit if you have the time. A monastic community was established here early in the fifth century when monks first inhabited the caves in the cliff face. The monastery itself was built later, only to be destroyed in 614 by Persians invading the Holy Land. It was rebuilt in 1173 and again in 1878. The Church of the Virgin Mary at the monastery contains many paintings and icons, and the Church of St John and St George nearby contains sixth-century mosaics and the skulls of monks martyred by the Persians. But of particular interest are the paintings in the cave above the monastery called the Grotto of Elijah. They commemorate the time when the prophet was fed by ravens in the wilderness. Further along the cliff, there are also fine twelfth-century frescoes in the cave of St John of Thebes, founder of this monastery. The paths to the caves lead in all directions on the cliff face.

The palaces of the Wadi Qilt

Continue past the monastery. Notice a high mound to the left of the road as it descends to the plain west of Jericho. On this mound, Herod the Great built a fortress called Cypros to protect his winter palace on the banks of the Wadi Qilt. It is worth stopping and climbing the mound to see the Herodian remains — the work of a king with a taste for the greatest possible luxury. Jerusalem is very cold in the winter months — snow is not unknown in the holy city. And it rains heavily at places like Masada or Machaerus (see Day 9) where Herod built his great palace-fortresses. So Herod chose to winter here by the Wadi Qilt because the climate is much more pleasant than elsewhere.

In the heyday of this palace, the buildings extended on both sides of the Wadi. A large reception hall and two colonnaded courts on the north bank were connected by a bridge to a sunken garden south of the Wadi. This is a desert setting today, but in Herod's time the palace, its baths and gymnasium, its gardens, swimming pool and surrounding orchards were watered by aqueducts. King Herod the Great died at this palace in 4 B.C., and the buildings were destroyed by the Romans at the end of the first Jewish revolt. It is possible to make a short detour through the suburbs of Jericho to the other side of the Wadi, where the remains can be seen at close quarters.

The remains of a Hasmonean palace built before Herod's time can also be seen west of the Herodian buildings — although it is not clear when this palace was built or who was responsible for building it. The Hasmonean palace consisted of a large main building, a pavilion and a swimming pool, divided by a broad ramp into two halves and surrounded by a spacious court. The Hasmonean and the Herodian palaces at the Wadi Qilt have recently been excavated.

Continue along the main route into Jericho.

Jericho

Modern Jericho lies within an oasis about eight miles north of the Dead Sea, close to the desert cliffs which hang over the west side of the rift valley. Sub-tropical plants and brightly coloured flowers abound, and the fruit stalls sell newly picked bananas and plump avocado pears. Oranges, lemons and grapefruit grow in the orchards which line the streets. This Arab town of about seven thousand inhabitants makes two claims to fame. It is certainly the lowest urban settlement on the surface of the earth, eight hundred and twenty feet below sea level. And it is said to be the most ancient city in the world — although the modern town lies about a mile southeast of the tel. The main industry at Jericho is agriculture, however there are also several shops which specialize in bedsteads, trays, kettles and other artifacts made in brass and copper. There are several fruit stalls and restaurants on the road north towards the tel. It is worth stopping the car. The fresh fruit of Jericho is not to be missed — nowhere else do bananas taste like this! Afterwards, return to the car and move on to the tel.

Many archaeologists have worked on the tel at Jericho, but the most remarkable discoveries were made in the 1950s by the British archaeologist Kathleen Kenyon. Most of the archaeological information detailed below comes from Kathleen Kenyon's report on the site. However, what the visitor can see here tells only half the story. Many fascinating finds from the shrines and tombs of ancient Jericho are preserved at the Israel Museum in Jerusalem (to be visited on Day 8).

The ancient city, near a crossing place of the River Jordan, was always liable to attack from the east — and was therefore influenced by many cultures. The word 'Jericho' means 'moon', no doubt because moon worship took place here. Access to the site of the ancient city is from the car park south of the tel. Notice the mudbrick walls. They belong to pre-biblical Jericho, yet they are not dissimilar to the mudbrick walls of the Palestinian refugee camp nearby. Below the tel to the right is Ein es-Sultan, this was the spring which first led people to settle here and which continues to water the palm trees and the orchards of the oasis.

The history of Jericho begins with a shrine built near the spring in about 9,500 B.C. — probably because the spring was regarded as holy. It belonged to nomadic hunters who ranged far and wide and who returned here from time to time. Progress was slow, but by about 8,000 B.C. domed circular houses of mudbrick had been built at Jericho. Mankind had yet to learn the art of making pottery — cups and dishes used in this period were carved out of limestone. No doubt utensils were also made of wood and other materials, but only limestone has survived. To support a population of about two thousand inhabitants, the oasis at Jericho was extended by irrigation.

In the earliest centuries, Jericho was undefended by city walls. Sometime between 8,000 and 7,000 B.C., a thick city wall of rough stones and a massive stone tower were built. Notice the deep section which has been cut into the tel to expose the stone tower. The tower looks ordinary enough, but it has certainly surprised the experts. It was built long before such constructions were even thought possible — five thousand years earlier than the first Egyptian pyramid.

The city was overthrown with great violence in about 7000 B.C., by no means an unusual event in the story of Jericho. Time and time again, a long period of settled urban life was interrupted by the arrival of migrants who destroyed the city. Afterwards, the tel was sometimes deserted for centuries. The site was usually resettled by primitive tribes living in tents or pits in the ground. It took centuries for urban life to develop once more.

Evidence has been found of the religious ideas of some of the people who lived there. A carefully worked stone pillar was found, for instance, from the seventh millennium B.C. Such pillars were meant to encourage the fertility of crops, animals and wives. And ten human skulls were discovered from the same period, used for some form of ancestor worship. The features of the dead had been skilfully restored in plaster and painted in natural colours, their eyes replaced with shells. One of these skulls is preserved at the Ashmolean Museum, Oxford.

Discoveries from the tombs of ancient Jericho are also very interesting. In the later periods, the dead were laid fully clothed on beds or rush mats, bone-decorated wooden combs in their hair, wearing rings and pendants. Bone-decorated boxes and alabaster vessels were also found in these tombs — the discoveries at Jericho have greatly extended our knowledge of Canaanite civilization.

The city was destroyed by fire and great violence in about 1560 B.C. The tel was not re-occupied until about 1400 B.C. But the remains of the final Canaanite city at Jericho, very likely encountered by the invading Israelites under Joshua, are scanty indeed. The famous biblical story tells how the walls of Jericho collapsed at the coming of the Israelites. It can neither be proved nor disproved — centuries of erosion have washed the remains of it away.

Detour

The tel affords a fine view of a Greek Orthodox monastery called Qarantal, built halfway up the cliffs west of Jericho (a short drive of about ½ mile). Most people were attracted to Jericho by the fertility of the oasis. But a solitary life of prayer attracted the anchorites of the fourth century who chose as their refuge inaccessible caves in the cliffs. Later, a monastery called Douka was built at the top of these cliffs. It was destroyed in the seventh century, and the present monastery was built towards the end of the nineteenth century. The name is derived from the Latin 'Quarantena', meaning forty, and is based on the tradition that this was the mountain on which Jesus spent forty days and nights in the wilderness. Qarantal and the site of Douka can be reached by a path which leads from the base of the cliffs. The view from the top is breathtaking.

Drive about a mile and a half northeast of the tel at Jericho to Hisham's Palace.

Hisham's Palace

It was built at the beginning of his reign by Hisham, the tenth Umayyad caliph who rules the Muslim empire from A.D. 724 to 743. This royal complex set in a centre of great agricultural wealth was typical of the period. Yet it survived only a short time. The buildings suffered from an earthquake in 746, and were covered in sand until excavated by English archaeologists in 1937.

The remains of the palace offer many insights into early Islamic architecture and art. A gatehouse leads from the forecourt into the central courtyard. These were the domestic quarters of the palace, with rooms at ground and first-floor level. Notice the circular stone window — it once belonged to one of the rooms overlooking the courtyard but now stands at the centre of it.

To the north are the remains of a number of public buildings. Large areas of fine Islamic mosaic have been excavated — when this palace was built, the mosaic floors extending in all directions must have looked like vast areas of rich carpeting. Nearly all the mosaics exhibit geometric designs, but inside in a small apse in the large bath house is one of the treasures of the palace. A perfectly preserved mosaic depicts an orange tree beneath which are two gazelles, one being attacked by a lion. The warm colours and fine craftsmanship give a glimpse of the richness with which this palace was once ornamented. The bath house was a hall of pleasure — a place for music and dancing. Perhaps it was also used for formal receptions. Alongside the bath house, there are also the remains of the palace mosque.

After leaving Hisham's Palace, follow Route 90 through Jericho into the desert. Soon the northern extremity of the Dead Sea lies on the left. To the right a few miles further on, the remains of the monastery of Qumran stand on a rocky plinth below cliffs honeycombed with caves.

Qumran

Temperatures in the desert are likely to be high, but there is an airconditioned restaurant at Qumran beside the site. There is no settlement at Qumran.

Lunch at Qumran.

Once on the site itself, begin by passing through the excavations. On the right, on the other side of a deep wadi, is the keyhole-shaped entrance to Cave 4, where was found the bulk of the library known as the Dead Sea Scrolls. It is said that a bedouin boy found the scrolls while searching for a lost goat — made up, I think, by a scholar who wanted a good story for the newspapers. But the truth is no less interesting. In the 1940s before the partition of Palestine, many goods were much cheaper in Transjordan. The bedouins regularly smuggled rice, sugar, coffee, carpets and other commodities across the Jordan. But the British authorities were well aware of it and patrolled the roads. When the smugglers were in danger of being caught, they hid their contraband in the caves. In 1947 during one of these expeditions, a Ta'amreh bedouin came across jars inside a cave in the valley of the Dead Sea — not on the usual route of the smugglers, otherwise the scrolls might have been found sooner. As will be seen at Petra (p. 143), the bedouins are always looking for treasure. But the contents of the jar looked like a bundle of old rags — hardly the silver and gold of the bedouin imagination. The find consisted of a long roll of ancient brown leather on which there was writing in parallel columns. The bedouin had no idea that he was looking at a priceless manuscript — a copy of the book of Isaiah a thousand years earlier than any other copy to have survived into the modern world.

The story of the discovery of many other priceless manuscripts in these caves, and the way in which the Dead Sea Scrolls finally arrived in the hands of the scholars, reads like a novel full of intrigue. Some people made fortunes out of the discovery. It was virtually impossible for scholars to visit the region of the Dead Sea — this was the period of the partition of Palestine, when the Israelis and the Arabs fought for the Holy Land. Scrolls and parts of scrolls passed from dealer to dealer as the bedouins discovered and sold them. Eventually it was established that a monastery of a Jewish sect called the Essenes existed at Qumran in the first century, and that their library had been stored in the caves nearby — probably when the Romans retook the Holy Land in 70 B.C. at the end of the first Jewish revolt.

Notice how inaccessible Cave 4 was — the monks evidently did not want the Romans to find their library. Then examine the remains of the monastery itself. Modern books are printed on paper, quired and bound. But the books of the first century were handwritten on parchment or papyrus, and took the form of scrolls. A new copy was laboriously written out by hand, word by word and page by page — the work of the professional scribes. Visit the Scriptorium where this work was done. The scribes wrote in ink, using reed pens, copying from one long strip of material to another. In the remains of this room, the archaeologists found ceramic inkwells and long wooden tables with plastered tops.

To enable such a book to be read, each end of the scroll was wound around a wooden handle — the reader twisted the handles to move from page to page. Modern books are stored in rows on shelves. But the scroll books were wrapped in linen and kept in earthenware jars. You can see the remains of the kiln where the jars were fired. The scrolls themselves can be seen in Jerusalem at the Shrine of the Book (see p. 134).

Ein Gedi

About twenty miles south of Qumran is the large oasis of Ein Gedi — usually one of the hottest places in the Holy Land. There is an airconditioned restaurant, but the other way to keep cool is to bathe in the Dead Sea — an experience not to be missed. The water is viscous, leaving small bubbles on the skin, reputed to be therapeutic. (Further south, there are health farms where ample ladies wallow in the Dead Sea mud — a unique entertainment of the region.) It's not really possible to swim. You float about like an amoeba in a stagnant pond.

Continue about eleven miles south to Masada.

Masada

The remains of the great palace-fortress of Herod the Great at Masada are to be found at the top of a great mountain spur. This magnificent complex of palaces and fortifications was excavated in 1963 and 1964 by the Israeli archaeologist Yigael Yadin, assisted by a vast army of volunteers from all over the world. The dramatic story of their discoveries is told in Yadin's *Masada*, first published in 1966.

The road to Masada leads to the right off Route 90. At the base of the mountain are bus stops, restaurants, a youth hostel and the terminal for the cable car which takes visitors to the top. Alternatively, visitors can take the 'Snake' Path, so called because it snakes up the mountain. The atmosphere on Masada is very dry — visitors should take plenty of liquids. Notice the little black and yellow birds called Tristram's Grackle. They will eat the cheese from your sandwiches — not the bread, they are very discriminating.

It would be easy to spend several days investigating Masada, but certain features are not to be missed. Turn right at the top and head for the remains of the great hanging palaces which are a feature of this fortress. Masada had been fortified long before the time of Herod the Great. But as elsewhere he demanded a life of great luxury within the desert fortress. The palaces are on three levels carved out of the rock, now connected by a modern staircase which descends over the cliff face. At the lowest level are the remains of a large rectangular palace, ornamented with elegant pillars and pilasters, the walls plastered and marbled. Astonishingly, some of the interior decor from Herod's time has survived.

At the second level are the remains of a rotunda, while at the apex of the great rock are the remains of a palace fronted by a portico and a wide balcony.

Many other fascinating discoveries from the time of Herod the Great have been made at Masada. The long narrow store rooms to the west of the hanging palaces, for instance, yielded up a variety of commodities preserved by the desert and still recognizable over two thousand years later — salt, grain, olives, pomegranates, walnuts and dates. And it's worth visiting one of the vast cisterns which supplied the fortress with water. In the winter season, millions of gallons of water were carried up to the top of the rock in leather buckets to fill these cisterns. But the story of Masada is not simply that of the fortress built by King Herod the Great. The first act of the Jewish revolt against the Romans came in A.D. 66, when the Jewish zealots climbed Masada, probably at night, and slaughtered the Roman garrison. And when the Romans retook the Holy Land, the last stand of the zealots was at Masada.

Look down at the desert below the hanging palaces. The remains of square Roman forts can be seen lying there as well as the wall which the legionaries built all round Masada to trap the defenders. The largest fort was the headquarters of Silva, the Roman general in charge of operations. Visit, too, the remains of the casemate walls overhanging the south cliff face — where people coming from the cable car arrive at the top. The use of casemate walls was common long before Herod's time — small rooms were built inside the walls, creating a large flat roof on which defenders could be massed. But at the time of the siege of Masada, these small rooms were occupied by the zealots and their families. The excavations have yielded fascinating glimpses of these patriots of the first century — eye-shadow, for instance, make-up brushes and bottles of perfume used by the women. When the Romans laid siege to Masada in the winter of A.D. 72, nine hundred and sixty men, women and children, led by a commander called Eleazar, were there to resist them.

And how did the Romans retake Masada? Look at the remains of the great ramp built by the legionaries against the north side of the rock. To hold this ramp together, a wooden structure was built. Then rubble, carried in baskets, was piled up to a height of over six hundred feet — a task which took months to complete. And when it was complete, a tower full of troops with a battering ram was winched up the side of Masada to attack the perimeter walls of the fortress. After that, it was only a matter of time. And what happened to the zealots? When the legionaries broke in, they were greeted by an unearthly silence. The zealots had not been prepared to fall into Roman hands. Every man had killed his family. Then his neighbour had killed him. Only a couple of women and some small children hidden in a cave lived to tell the tale.

The role which Masada played in history did not, however, completely cease with the recapture of the fortress. Later, the great rock was taken over by anchorites who sought contemplation and prayer in the silences of the desert. Their memorial is a fine Byzantine church at Masada.

After the visit to Masada, return to Jerusalem on Route 90 and Route 1.

Overnight at Jerusalem.

Opening Times

The tel at Jericho and Hisham's Palace (tel: 02-922522) are open daily, 8 a.m. – 5 p.m. There is a small museum at the entrance to the palace. Admission to Qumran (tel: 02-922505) is also 8 a.m. – 5 p.m. At Masada (tel: 057-90907), the cable car stops working at 4 p.m.

A Selection of Restaurants in Jericho
El Gandool, a good Arab restaurant on the road to the tel

Rowda, signposted to the right as you enter Jericho, good value

Maxim, self-service restaurant, near Zachaeus' tree

There are several four- and five-star hotels on the Dead Sea coast which serve good but expensive meals.

There are also self-service restaurants on site at Qumran and Masada.

JERICHO: USEFUL INFORMATION

Population:	7,000
Altitude:	820 ft below sea level
Facilities:	restaurants and archaeological sites

Jerusalem 24 miles

EIN GEDI: USEFUL INFORMATION

Government Tourist Information Office: Shopping Centre, Arad (tel: 57 98144)

Facilities:	bathing beach on the Dead Sea, Ein Fashcha nature reserve

Jerusalem 57 miles

MASADA: USEFUL INFORMATION

Government Tourist Information Office: Beer Sheva (tel: 57 36001)

Facilities:	archaeological site

Jerusalem 68 miles

79

The aquaduct built by Herod the Great for Caesarea Maritima

DAY 4

Jerusalem, Netanya, Caesarea Maritima, Tiberias: approximately 125 miles

Leaving Jerusalem, go north to Galilee. But on the way visit Netanya, a popular Israeli coastal resort on the Plain of Sharon. Relax after visiting the series of archaeological sites on Day 3. The bathing beaches are clean, sandy and extensive at Netanya. In the afternoon, follow the coastal highway to visit Caesarea Maritima, a city built by Herod the Great and further developed in the Byzantine and Crusader periods. Then skirt Mount Carmel and drive through the Turan Valley to Tiberias on the shores of the Sea of Galilee. Overnight at Tiberias.

Map references

Netanya	134:193
Caesarea Maritima	140:212
Carmel Caves	148:231
Tiberias	201:242

Route shown p. 112.

Breakfast in Jerusalem.

Leave Jerusalem westwards following Route 1. Notice the way in which precipitous mountain slopes surround the holy city. Alongside the modern highway, you will see here and there the remains of antique military vehicles, the relics of the 1948 struggles between Arab and Jew. General Sir Edward Allenby also fought the Turks along this route in 1917. As George Adam Smith, the great nineteenth-century Scottish student of the Holy Land said of this approach to Jerusalem through the Vale of Ajalon, 'It is a country of ambushes, entanglements, surprises, where large armies have no room to fight and the defenders can remain hidden; where the essentials for war are nimbleness and the sure foot, the power of scramble and of rush.' When Allenby discovered that the Roman roads marked on his maps had long been reduced to mere tracks, he abandoned his military vehicles and the campaign continued using camels.

Gradually the hill country gives way to the coastal plain of the Holy Land. On the outskirts of Tel Aviv, go right onto Route 4 which runs through the Plain of Sharon, an extensive alluvial plateau which stretches from the foothills of Samaria to the Mediterranean coast. The word 'Sharon' means 'the forest' — there are still clumps of stunted oak trees to be seen in the north, but nowadays the terrain is subject to intensive agriculture. There are banana plantations, fields of wheat, cotton and tobacco. Orchards of orange, lemon and grapefruit abound, and here and there large fish ponds have been dug. In ancient times, this was largely an inhospitable mixture of forest and swamp, known also for its brightly coloured wild flowers although, disappointingly, the nubile Shulamite's description of herself in The Song of Songs as 'the rose of Sharon' has more recently been translated as 'the crocus of the plain'. On reaching Route 57, go left for Netanya.

Netanya

There is little to say about Netanya except that it is a popular holiday resort with good hotels, restaurants and beaches. The town came into existence in the 1920s and was named in honour of Nathan Straus, turn-of-the-century New York businessman and philanthropist who gave a great deal of money to various Jewish projects in health and child welfare in the Holy Land. During World War II, immigrants from Antwerp set up the diamond-polishing industry at Netanya. This is a morning for lazing on the beach followed, perhaps, by a good lunch. But the diamond workshops and exhibition rooms in the south of the town are worth visiting. Afterwards continue north, taking Route 2, the coastal highway, and turn off for Caesarea Maritima.

Caesarea Maritima

The Mediterranean seaboard of the Holy Land sweeps without natural harbours in a regular line from Haifa to Gaza because a ridge of black basalt runs the whole length of the coast. It was one of the problems which faced Herod the Great in 22 B.C. when he began to build a new port near an old Phoenician naval station called Strato's Tower on the coast of the Plain of Sharon. To overcome it, Herod's engineers constructed a great mole based on huge stones, built in an arc out to sea to enclose the harbour — they even used a concrete which would set under water. Herod called his new port Caesarea in honour of Caesar Augustus the Roman Emperor, and built a magnificent temple to Augustus on a high platform overlooking the harbour. In it was a colossal statue of the Emperor.

Herod also built a new walled city at Caesarea, with neatly planned streets and squares — it even included a sewage system which carried waste products from the city out to sea. There was a hippodrome for chariot-racing, and a large theatre south of the city. Caesarea was Herod's idea of a city, Greek in concept, sumptuous, well-appointed and furnished with lavish entertainments of all kinds.

The archaeological remains which can be seen today at Caesarea Maritima date from many periods from the time of Herod the Great to the Crusades. This is one of the most attractive archaeological sites in the Holy Land, standing on the Mediterranean coast. People visit the site in large numbers and patronize the beach either side — also a resort for sea fishing. There are three main sources of archaeological interest — the Herodian theatre, the walled city and the Herodian aqueduct. There is no modern city at Caesarea Maritima.

Visit first the remains of Herod's theatre, at a junction where the road through the sand dunes turns north in the direction of the ancient city itself. This is probably the best example of a classical theatre to be found in the Holy Land — it has been reconstructed and is now used for orchestral concerts. Stand in the middle of the stage and whisper — it's astonishing how well the sound is conveyed. It's not unusual for tourists to burst into song in the remains of this theatre from the first century B.C.

After Herod's time, Caesarea became the Roman administrative centre of Judea. During the excavations, a stone has been discovered with the inscription, 'Pontius Pilatus, Praefactus Judaeae' — Pilate was prefect A.D. 26-36 The New Testament tells us that St Peter baptized a Roman centurion called Cornelius at Caesarea, and St Paul was brought here as a prisoner to be questioned by Felix who was prefect A.D. 52-60. Later, Caesarea became an important centre of Christianity.

By the end of the second century the city was the seat of a bishop and the episcopal library was a famous centre of learning. The archaeologists have discovered evidence of a large public building which was destroyed in the seventh century when the Arabs captured the city. The site today is occupied by part of the Crusader moat. A statue of the Good Shepherd and sections of mosaic floor from this building have been recovered — it therefore seems likely that this was the famous library. Unlike the Dead Sea Scrolls preserved at the Shrine of the Book in Jerusalem (see Day 8) many of the manuscript books at this library were quired and bound like modern books. The library contained books both ranged on shelves and in scroll form, stored in jars.

The most important work to be carried out at the library was Origen's *Hexapla* which contained six versions of the Old Testament in parallel columns. The early Church knew little of the Hebrew Old Testament — Hebrew was already a dead language in the first century. Greek was the international language of the period, and the early Church relied on a Greek translation for its knowledge of the Old Testament. But, in the *Hexapla*, Origen supplied the Christian scholars of his time with a copy of the Old Testament in the original Hebrew together with various Greek versions of the text. His work was completed in A.D. 245 and was so voluminous that it was never re-copied in its entirety.

A glimpse of Caesarea Maritima in the Byzantine period can be seen in the excavations opposite the entrance to the main archaeological site. Notice the wide street and the elegant statues — Byzantine Caesarea was much more extensive than the Herodian city. The Muslims took Caesarea in 639, and it remained in their hands for four hundred years. The city was not attacked at the beginning of the first Crusade but, in 1101, Baldwin I captured the city and slaughtered the inhabitants.

Study the fine Crusader fortifications which surround the remains of the walled city. The Crusaders learnt a great deal about the art of fortification from the ancient cities of the Holy Land. It was common, for instance, to create a 'glacis' whereby the sides of the mound below the defensive walls of a city were covered in a slippery plaster. The shelving Crusader walls descending into the moat at Caesarea are reminiscent of the glacis found at such cities as Hazor (see p. 102-3). These fortifications at Caesarea were the work of King Louis IX of France in 1251. The city was then held by the Crusaders until 1265.

Within the Crusader walls are the remains of buildings from many different periods — Herodian, Roman, Byzantine, Arab and Crusader. There are also interesting craft shops and restaurants. The present harbour dates from the Crusader period — the Herodian harbour stretched much further out to sea. But here and there the remains of Herod's gigantic mole can be detected beneath the water.

A visit to the aqueduct north of the archaeological site is also very rewarding — it involves a walk through the sand dunes. Two thousand years after it was built, the aqueduct constructed by the builders of King Herod the Great continues to stand high above the sea shore. Follow the aqueduct on its shore side for about a hundred yards. An inscription can be seen cut into the masonry above an arch, recording repairs carried out by the legionaries in the time of the Emperor Hadrian.

On leaving Caesarea Maritima, go eastwards and turn north on Route 4 which runs parallel to the coastal highway.

The Carmel Caves

Visit the Carmel Caves in the foothills of the Carmel Range. Mount Carmel is associated with the Old Testament conflict between Elijah and the prophets of Baal. But in these caves, the archaeologists have found evidence of human habitation infinitely older than anything found in the Old Testament.

Drive into the Valley of the Caves, a narrow cleft in the foothills of the Carmel Range. The caves hang at various heights in the southern escarpment of the valley. It is a scramble through the prickly pears about eighty feet up a rough track to reach the highest of them, called the Cave of the Oven. These large caves were formed by water cutting into the porous limestone. But the flow of water had ceased and people were already living in the caves perhaps as long as thirty thousand years ago.

Walk into the Cave of the Oven. It consists of a large central chamber. A funnel formed by the water rises through the rock above — used by the cave dwellers as a natural chimney. Imagine a small group of primitive men, women and children, dressed in animal skins, sitting around a large fire beneath the funnel. That fire kept them warm at night, and they used it for cooking. The archaeologists have found debris fifty feet in depth in the floor of the chamber, left by the people who lived here — much of it ash from the fires they made. But they have also found bones — hippopotamus, gazelle, horse, ox, fallow deer and other animals. The deepest levels were left by the earliest people of the cave. The bones showed what types of animals were caught for food at different times. There came a point, for instance, when large primitive animals were no longer available — the types of animals caught by the cave-dwellers also show that the climate changed several times. Many implements were found in these caves, especially flint scrapers used for a variety of purposes. A flint scraper, for instance, could shape the wooden shaft of an arrow, while a thinner, pointed sliver of flint could then be used as an arrow head.

People lived in the caves at the time when they survived by hunting. In the last period of human habitation, however, the remains of very early primitive buildings have been found on the terrace in front of the Cave of the Valley. They show that people were at last moving out of the caves. New types of implement began to be used — particularly sickles shaped out of flint, showing that people were beginning to plant and to harvest crops. The sickles were fitted with bone hafts and on many of them animal heads were carved. They are preserved at the Israel Museum in Jerusalem. This is the earliest form of art discovered in the caves, but the standard of workmanship is of excellent quality.

The caves have supplied fascinating insights into the very early development of human society — glimpses of the ideas and the art of those primitive cave-dwellers, and the way in which they lived. Such people could not expect to live very long lives. No skeleton of a man or a woman over the age of forty has been found. Most of our knowledge of primitive man has been gained from this part of the Middle East.

Haifa

Follow the main road north through Haifa, a city largely built on steep mountain sides where the Carmel Range descends to the sea. At sea level this is a busy port, but notice the modern high-rise buildings on Mount Carmel overlooking magnificent views of the coast. When the pharoah Pepi I went on a campaign north on the Way of the Sea in 2350 B.C., he instructed the Egyptian navy which followed his progress to land north of the headland at Haifa — which he called 'the Antelope's Nose'.

On leaving Haifa, take Route 75 north of the Carmel Range and turn left onto Route 77 which leads through the Turan Valley in the direction of the Sea of Galilee. Unlike the Holy Land generally in which the physical features run north-south, the land north of Carmel extends in huge plains interrupted by ranges of intermittent hills flowing east-west. From time immemorial, the road running through the Turan Valley came from the port at Akko (see p. 119) and linked the two great international highways of the Middle East, the Way of the Sea and the King's Highway in Transjordan. It crossed the Way of the Sea in the vicinity of Mount Tabor and, after descending into the Jordan valley, it climbed eastward up the deep Yarmuk gorge. During the Middle Ages, the same road linked the Far East to Europe. Products from the east, much prized in Europe, were brought this way and shipped from Akko.

Descend at last on the modern switchback road which snakes down to Tiberias in the rift valley by the Sea of Galilee.

Overnight at Tiberias.

Museums
The **Netanya Diamond Centre**, 90 Herzl Street (tel: 34624) is open Sunday-Thursday 8 a.m.-7 p.m., Friday 8 a.m.-2 p.m., Saturday closed.

A Selection of Hotels

Tiberias Plaza, five star, Waterfront, P.O. Box 375 (tel: 792233)

Galei Kinneret, five star, Kaplan Avenue (tel: 792331)

Ganei Hamad, four star, Habanim Street (tel: 792890) — interesting because, as at Hammath Tiberias, there are hot springs here and the hotel has its own lakeside beach

Golan Hotel, four star, 14 Achad Ha'am Street (tel: 791901)

Ron Beach, four star, Lakeside Road, P.O. Box 173 (tel: 721418) — beach-side swimming pool

Tzameret Inn, three star, P.O. Box 200 (tel: 794951) — in splendid isolation high on the hill above Tiberias

Holiday Hotel, three star, Gedud Barak Road (tel: 721901)

Tiberias, three star, 19 Obel Ya'akov Street (tel: 792270)

But in many ways the most pleasant, if not the least expensive, place to stay is **Nof Ginosar** (tel: 98878), a beach-side motel within a kibbutz north of Tiberias — recommended as a stopping place on Day 5 of these travels.

A Selection of Restaurants

Restaurant Renaissance, Ha'atzma'ut Square, Netanya (tel: 28653)

Taipei, Ha'atzma'ut Square, Netanya (tel: 28145)

Quiet Beach, Gedud Barak Road, Tiberias (tel: 720602)

An enjoyable excursion by boat over the Sea of Galilee will take you to the **Ein Gev Restaurant** on the kibbutz on the eastern side of the lake — specializes in dairy food.

There are many pavement restaurants in the town centre at Netanya and beach-side hotels which also serve non-residents.

Tiberias is famous for its fish restaurants along the promenade.

The **Fish on the Roof** at the Tiberias Plaza (tel: 792233) is probably the best, but expensive.

Chinese food: **The House**, Gedud Barak Road, Tiberias (tel: 792353)

NETANYA: USEFUL INFORMATION

Population:	105,000
Altitude:	66 ft
Facilities:	hotels, restaurants, beaches, diamond centre

Jerusalem 57 miles

TIBERIAS: USEFUL INFORMATION

Israeli Government Tourist Office, 8 Alhadess Street (tel: 720992)

Population:	27,000
Altitude:	696 ft below sea level
Facilities:	hotels, restaurants, beaches and marinas, pleasure craft, hot springs

Netanya 64 miles

The remains of the Synagogue at Capernaum

DAY 5

Tiberias, the Sea of Galilee, Capernaum, Chorazin and Tiberias: approximately 29 miles

The great contrasts of scenery in the Holy Land are no more evident than here — they range from the deserts of the south to this luxuriant countryside around the Sea of Galilee. People come to this region for their holidays. But this is also the world in which the ideas of the New Testament were first taught, and where Judaism recovered vitality after the failure of the successive Jewish revolts against imperial Rome. After a short early morning drive by the lakeside, explore Tiberias. See the remains of the superb synagogues at Hammath Tiberias, once the seat of the Sanhedrin. Head north around the lake, perhaps lunching on the way, to visit Capernaum where Jesus of Nazareth first centred his ministry — at least four of his disciples were Galilean fishermen. Visit too Chorazin, a Galilean city much restored to give a good impression of life in the first few centuries. Return to Tiberias.

Map references

Netanya	125:194
Capernaum	204:254
Chorazin	203:257

Route shown p. 112.

The Sea of Galilee

> O Sabbath rest by Galilee!
> O calm of hills above,
> Where Jesus knelt to share with thee
> The silence of eternity
> Interpreted by love!

The words of John Greenleaf Whittier, American shoemaker, Quaker and poet, have reverberated through a thousand school halls and are sung at endless society weddings. Most of the time he is right. On the other side of the lake from Tiberias, the Golan Heights hang above the eastern shore — the hills above are calm and the lake is serene. Yet one wonders whether the poet ever came here to see it, or whether his vision has more to do with the silences of the Quaker house of Boston, Massachusetts, than with this lake. The Sea of Galilee is also well known for its storms. The hot air rises out of the deep basin of the rift valley, and the cold air rushes down from the hills to replace it. The effect is a sudden and violent turbulence of wind and water. As the gospels tell us, these storms die down as quickly as they arise.

Green hills, wooded in places, descend to the lake on all sides. North of Tiberias the scene is dominated by Mount Arbel, honeycombed with caves. The lakeside fields are rich in crops of cotton, tobacco, wheat and maize. Begin early in the morning, perhaps before breakfast, by taking the lakeside road north out of Tiberias. As in New Testament times, many of the fishing boats on the Sea of Galilee return to land in the early morning after a night's fishing, so this is the best time to watch them. The road runs along the lakeside until it comes to Magdala, thought to be the home village of Mary Magdalene. It's worth stopping to watch the fishing boats straggled across the lake — often a boat can be seen working inshore. The lake lies about six hundred feet below sea level, its fresh water well-stocked with fish, notably 'musht' — now usually called 'St Peter's fish' — which is found only in these waters. It is characterized by its wide, flat shape and its long dorsal fin. Sometimes, two boats can be seen fishing together — a scene typical of New Testament times. The fishermen put out their nets in exactly the same way as they did in the first century, except that their boats are now equipped with outboard motors.

Further on, the road leaves the lakeside and runs through the Plain of Gennesaret, a coastal strip of great fertility on the western shore. Products native to the Holy Land such as wheat, olives and pomegranates are grown here. One could well believe that, when Jesus told the story of the Parable of the Sower 'beside the sea', a farmer was at work sowing his seed in a nearby field. The sonorous prose of the Authorized Version disguises the comedy of the story. 'Don't you think he's a fool,' asked Jesus, 'throwing valuable seed away like that?' But practically any crop can be grown in the Plain of Gennesaret. There are banana plantations on the lakeside, and fields of cotton, maize and tobacco.

Return to Tiberias for breakfast.

Tiberias and Hammath Tiberias

Walk along the lakeside promenade at Tiberias, now a popular holiday resort famous for its fish restaurants. A small marina full of pleasure boats gives way to a paved quayside verging on garden restaurants with lights hanging in the trees and the occasional waft of Israeli pop music — very similar to western pop, except that in oriental fashion the voices waver around the note. In the background, nearer the town centre, large modern hotels, mostly expensive, dominate the sky-line. There seem to be few old buildings in Tiberias. Yet the original city was built a little to the south of the modern town, founded in A.D. 20 by Herod Antipas, ruler of Galilee, one of the sons of King Herod the Great. It was named in honour of Tiberias, the Roman Emperor. Antipas, like his father, represented Roman power and Greek culture, a figure mistrusted and disliked by his subjects. He chose to site his city here because it stood at the confluence of important roads — the route up the Jordan valley from Jericho and the route through the Turan valley from the port at Akko. From Tiberias the trade route ran north to Capernaum and, ultimately, to Damascus. The strict religious Jews of the time would not enter Tiberias, because they said that ancient graves had been desecrated when the new city was built.

Follow the lakeside road south in the direction of Hammath Tiberias, nowadays on the outskirts of the town. Natural hot springs are a notable feature of Hammath Tiberias — originally, the city was simply called 'Hammath' meaning 'hot springs'. In the early Israelite period, this was a fortress of the tribe of Napthali controlling the lakeside road. Bath houses were built around the springs during the Roman period, when they were a source of income since the waters were believed to possess healing powers.

Tiberias and Hammath Tiberias merged, probably later in the first century, although they continued to maintain separate identities. The modern bath houses at Hammath are on the same site as those of the Roman period. There is also a large, well-appointed sports centre where it is possible to buy refreshments. Outside, a steaming-hot fountain rises from the springs.

Hammath Tiberias became an important centre of Judaism in the second century when many Judean Jews fled to Galilee after the suppression of the successive Jewish revolts against Roman power. This was a period of crisis for the Jewish religion. The Temple in Jerusalem had been destroyed by the Romans in A.D. 70. Synagogues had been in existence for some time — Jesus of Nazareth attended both the local synagogue and the Temple of Jerusalem — but the destruction of the Temple led to a new emphasis on the synagogue and the study of the scriptures which took place within its walls. During this period, the books of scriptures to be included in the Old Testament were selected by Jewish scholars. After the destruction of the Temple, the Sanhedrin — the ruling council of Judaism — was reconstituted away from Jerusalem. In the third century, Hammath was the seat of the Sanhedrin.

The archaeologists have discovered the remains of a series of synagogues built at different times on the same site at Hammath Tiberias. Notice that the buildings of the ancient city were built of the black basalt characteristic of Galilee, a product of the lava which flowed when the volcanoes of the Golan were active. Hot water from the springs flows through the archaeological site. The most strking remains are those of a fourth-century synagogue which include a series of fine mosaics much influenced in style by Graeco-Roman art. At times, the second Commandment which prohibited Jews from making 'graven images' was taken literally. No representations of living things were made. But in this period, the Commandment was differently interpreted. Particularly striking are the depictions of the signs of the zodiac and of the Ark of the Law flanked on either side by menorah. A recess in the wall of the synagogue was used as the ark, in which the scrolls of the scriptures were stored. These were brought out for public reading at the synagogue services.

After visiting Hammath Tiberias go to Capernaum, the centre of Jesus' Galilean ministry. It is possible to take a pleasure boat from Tiberias, otherwise drive north along the lakeside on Route 90. On the right as you pass through the Plain of Gennesaret is Nof Ginosar, a kibbutz on which there is a hotel and restaurant in pleasant lakeside surroundings — a good place for a midday meal. Afterwards, continue on the lakeside road and turn right onto Route 87 for Capernaum.

Capernaum

Capernaum is, today, an archaeological site in the grounds of a Franciscan monastery. The town appears in the Bible only in the gospels, as the place where Jesus began his ministry. Although the word 'kefar' of 'Kefar Nahaum' means a 'village', Capernaum was clearly a place of some size in the first century, an important and bustling centre of commerce on the road which linked Galilee, ruled by Herod Antipas, to the territory of his brother Philip, ruler of the Golan. In earlier times, the Way of the Sea had run north up the western side of the Upper Jordan Valley. But by the first century, the main road ran on the eastern side of the valley towards a new town built by Philip called Caesarea Philippi (see p. 107).

Clearly, Jesus could not have chosen a better place in Galilee from which to disseminate his teachings. Many of the inhabitants of Capernaum earned their living through agriculture or fishing, but there were many contacts with the outside world. Travelling merchants visited this border settlement, and there was a busy market. The population was probably a mixture of Jews and Gentiles — the gospels tell us that there were tax collectors at the village and a small Roman garrison.

The archaeological site at Capernaum has been excavated in recent years by the Franciscans, revealing the remains of a large synagogue built in limestone, groups of small domestic houses, and a large octagonal church built of basalt. A milestone from the time of the Emperor Hadrian found here gives evidence of the international route through Capernaum — it is on display near the remains of the synagogue.

The small houses and courtyards in which the ordinary people lived were grouped within a communal wall. This method of building islands of houses explains why Jesus taught 'beside the sea'. There was little room within the confines of such a group of houses for the large crowds which came to listen to him. The basalt gives the remains of these houses a dark appearance, but when people lived here they were almost certainly plastered and painted. The remains of the synagogue, partly restored by the archaeologists, show that more money was spent on this building than on any other at Capernaum.

It is the finest existing example of an early Galilean synagogue, consisting of a main prayer hall and an enclosed courtyard. In its heyday, this building dominated the surroundings, reflecting the Jewish rule that a synagogue should be on a higher level than the surrounding houses. Notice, as at the Lithostratos at Jerusalem (see p. 64), that board games have been scratched on the pavement of the courtyard of the synagogue.

There has been controversy about the dating of this synagogue. As has been pointed out, the interpretation of the Second Commandment which prohibited 'graven images' varied a great deal in the history of Israel. Since the synagogue at Capernaum was rich in decoration, it is reasonable to date the building in the third or fourth century. Later, attitudes changed yet again and all but one of the human figures which decorated this building were defaced. Study the stones from the synagogue ranged at the south wall of the site. They depict animals and birds, fruits and plants. There are also carvings with a particular religious significance — a mobile ark, a Star of David, a menorah and a ram's horn.

The remains of the octagonal building on the south part of the site nearest the lake are also interesting. There is a strong tradition claiming that this was the site of Peter's house. The gospels tells us that Peter was a married man and imply that Jesus used his house as his home at Capernaum. Certainly this group of houses was nearest the lakeside, and therefore likely to have been inhabited by fishermen.

The appearance of the site is confusing. The Franciscan archaeologists have uncovered the remains of the original group of houses and courtyards. But in the fourth century there appears to have been a plain single building on the site and, in the fifth century, the octagonal building. It suggests that, early in the Christian tradition, the house was venerated as Jesus' home and that, in due course, churches were built there. During the excavations, pieces of plaster and pottery have been found on which appear the names of Peter and Jesus as well as such Christian symbols as crosses, fish and boats. Visitors should not be surprised that a large church and a large synagogue should have coexisted at Capernaum. The Judaeo-Christians of the Holy Land in the first few centuries observed the customs of both religions.

The site at Capernaum also offers the visitor an opportunity to study the domestic equipment in everyday use in the first century and later. Querns of various kinds were used for the grinding of corn; there are olive crushers and presses. Capernaum was occupied until the end of the Byzantine period and was then probably destroyed during the Arab conquest of the Holy Land.

Detour

The Old Testament is closely related to the promised land of the Israelites. But Jesus and his teachings are not related to the Holy Land in the same way. He spoke of the birds of the air and the flowers of the field, but one does not need to know the birds and flowers of Galilee in order to understand him. And many of the places venerated by Christians are on supposed sites for which no actual evidence can be put forward. On the way back from Capernaum on Route 87, visit Tabgha where perhaps Jesus performed his miracle of feeding the five thousand. The Church of the Multiplication of the Loaves and Fishes was first built in the fourth century and contains fine mosaics dated from the middle of the fifth century.

Afterwards, re-join Route 90 and follow the road north as it rises above the Sea of Galilee. To the right along a small road is the Church of the Beatitudes, built in 1936 on a site where the Sermon on the Mount may have been preached. The church was designed by the Italian architect Barluzzi who was also responsible for the Church of the Agony in the Garden of Gesthemane (see Day 8). It is ornamented with fine modern mosaics and stands in a unique position overlooking the lake. Originally a Byzantine church stood here.

Turn right from Route 90 onto local road 8277 to find the remains of ancient Chorazin, about two and a half miles from the northern shore of the Sea of Galilee — not to be confused with the small modern settlement also called Korazin. The site of the ancient city stands at the top of a mountain side strewn with basalt rocks. Stop on the roadside before getting to the site. Watch the birds which take advantage of the air currents of the hillsides — fan-tailed and brown-necked ravens, buzzards and egrets searching round the cattle.

Chorazin

The archaeological site stands on the right-hand side of the road. Chorazin is mentioned in the New Testament with Capernaum and Bethsaida as places which Jesus condemned because the citizens refused to accept his teachings. But few remains have been excavated from that period, and Chorazin may well have been not much more than a village at the time. A major expansion of the city occurred after the suppression of the Cochba revolt in A.D. 135, when many Jews from Judea fled north and settled in Galilee.

The second-century city was built on a series of terraces. The highest terrace was given over to public buildings such as the synagogue — the archaeological exploration and restoration of the city has concentrated on this area. The synagogue is dated from the turn of the third century and shows that Chorazin was a thriving Jewish community. The plan of the main prayer hall is very .similar to that at Capernaum. The neo-Grecian facade, facing Jerusalem, was richly decorated and punctuated with three doorways. Inside, columns supported the roof and a seat ran round at the base of the walls. But, unlike the Capernaum synagogue, this building was of basalt. As at Capernaum, many stone carvings from the synagogue can be seen. On a frieze, there are scenes from daily life — the picking and treading of grapes, hunting, and many depictions of animals. There are also medallions in stone on which are various human figures and faces, among them the face of Medusa. Unlike the synagogue at Capernaum, many of the human figures which decorated this building have survived. There are also carvings with a religious significance, such as the Ark of the Law and the menorah.

On the same terrace as the synagogue are the remains of other public buildings, shops and large private dwellings. They give the visitor a good impression of a Galilean city in its heyday. The terraces below were densely populated with domestic buildings. Such amenities as a roofed-over water cistern and oil presses were found on the lowest terrace.

The history of the city was, however, stormy. Early in the fourth century, Eusebius, bishop of Caesarea, reports that Chorazin was in ruins. In the fifth century, it had been rebuilt. It was destroyed again at the end of the seventh or the beginning of the eighth century, and the site was deserted until the thirteenth century when it was resettled. Chorazin was again deserted in the fifteenth century.

Afterwards, return to Tiberias on Route 90.

Overnight at Tiberias.

For accommodation and restaurants in Tiberias, see p. 88-9.

SEA OF GALILEE: USEFUL INFORMATION

Altitude:	689 ft below sea level
Size:	7 miles wide, 13 miles long
Facilities:	beaches, pleasure cruises

This is also the largest fresh-water reservoir in the Holy Land — water is piped to irrigate the Negev in the south.

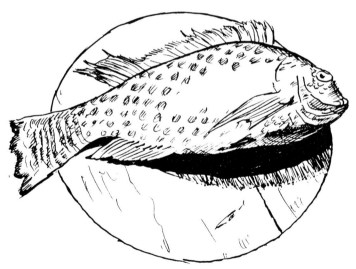

St. Peter's fish – only caught in the Sea of Galilee but served in fish restaurants throughout Israel

Canaanite mudbrick gateway at Dan

DAY 6

Tiberias, Hazor, Dan, Banias, Gamla, Tiberias: approximately 105 miles

A day trip from Tiberias. First visit the site of Hazor, in the Canaanite period one of the greatest cities in the Middle East. Then lunch at Dubrovin's Farm in the Huleh Valley — the Dubrovins were Russian farmers who emigrated here in the nineteenth century. See the astonishing mudbrick city gate which has survived from the Early Bronze Age at Tel Dan. Visit Banias, the shrine of the god Pan where Philip, ruler of the Golan in the first century, built his new city called Caesarea Philippi. Then see Gamla, where a city was built on the crest of a hill shaped like a camel's back. When the Romans took Gamla as they suppressed the Jewish revolt, they threw men, women and children down the precipitous slopes of the mountain. Return to Tiberias.

Map references
Hazor   203:269
Dan   211:294
Banias   215:294
Gamla   219:256

Route shown p. 112.

Breakfast at Tiberias

Follow Route 90 from Tiberias into the Upper Jordan Valley. This is part of the Way of the Sea. North of the Sea of Galilee the road climbs the Rosh Pinna Sill, created in prehistoric times by an immense flow of lava into the river valley when the volcanoes of the Golan were active. For many centuries the sill trapped the headwaters of the Jordan, creating Lake Huleh in the valley to the north. Later the river excavated a deep gorge for itself through the basalt, reducing the lake to vast tracts of malarial swamp.

Hazor

The remains of Hazor, twenty-two miles north of Tiberias, confront the road where it emerges from the basalt hills of the Rosh Pinna Sill into the wide open spaces of the Upper Jordan Valley. As in ancient times, the road curves round to skirt the tel. Nowadays, this is one of the most impressive archaeological sites in the Holy Land. In the Canaanite and Old Testament periods, many cities on the Way of the Sea linked Egypt with the Mesopotamian valley, but Hazor was the greatest of them. The north and south met here.

Stop on the roadway below the tel. Imagine this great city towards the end of the fourteenth century B.C. No labour or military skill had been spared in the construction of the gigantic defences of Hazor. The mudbrick walls of the citadel, three quarters of a mile all round, were twenty-five feet thick and rose a full forty feet above the highest point of the tel which, in turn, stood a hundred and twenty feet above the surrounding countryside.

But this city was not simply a fortress. It stood at a confluence of routes in the Upper Jordan Valley, the greatest trading city in the Middle East. Merchants with their pack camels and mules brought their wares to the markets of Hazor from Babylon, Persia and far-away India. The dates and palms of the oasis at Jericho supplied the market stalls. Mirrors and jewellery were on sale, made by the craftsmen of Egypt. Graceful pottery from the Greek islands came from the west through the Mediterranean ports of Tyre and Akko.

You can take your car up to the citadel. To the north, at a lower level shaped in an irregular square, lies the remains of the commercial quarter of the city. In the fourteenth century B.C., this was a world of meandering alleyways, bazaars and narrow streets. This lower city was also fortified with thick mudbrick walls — and look at the high man-made rampart which was raised to defend the western side of this commercial quarter. The archaeologists have discovered that a different defensive technique was used on the eastern side of the lower city. There, the walls and towers stood about forty-five feet above the surrounding countryside. Small stones were dug into the side of the mound below the walls and covered in a slippery layer of hard plaster — called a glacis. The technique was imitated by the Crusaders when they built the defences of Caesarea Maritima (see p. 85).

The Bible tells us that the Israelites under Joshua took Hazor in the mid-thirteenth century B.C. and burned the city with fire. The biblical stories of the Israelite invasion of the Holy Land often seem difficult to believe. The massive defences of Canaanite Hazor belie the idea that the Israelites took this city. Yet the excavations on the tel confirm the biblical account. In the mid-thirteenth century B.C., the lower city was destroyed never to be rebuilt. A thick layer of ash gives evidence of the fire started by the invaders. Afterwards, the magnificent buildings were replaced by primitive dwellings. The Israelites could take a city with the most sophisticated defences in the ancient world, but their building techniques lagged far behind their military brilliance.

The Israelites, though, learnt from the people they conquered. Since Hazor stood on an important trade and military route, it was soon necessary to refortify the city. A gate and wide casemate walls have been found from the time of Solomon. The remains of a large pillared storehouse from the time of Omri, King of Israel in the ninth century B.C. can be seen on the tel. But particularly striking from the Israelite period are the remains of the water system near the southern edge of the mound — probably from the time of Ahab, King of Israel in the ninth century B.C.

Descend into the water system from the citadel. The aim was to bring water into the city without going outside the fortifications. First, a vertical shaft was cut through the debris of previous generations on the mound. This consisted mostly of the remains of earlier mudbrick buildings. Then a sloping tunnel was quarried through the bedrock to a pool at the natural water level about a hundred feet below.

Hazor was taken and the city burnt down again in 732 B.C. by Tiglath-pileser III, King of Assyria. Afterwards, the tel was used only intermittently as the site of a lonely fort overlooking the Huleh Valley.

Visit also the elegant little museum at the entrance to Kibbutz Aylet Hashachar just north of the tel. Of particular interest are discoveries from the remains of a Canaanite temple in the lower city — very similar in plan to the Temple built in Jerusalem centuries later. Outside, stood a 'high place' — a platform on which sacrifices were offered. The walls of the temple itself were decorated with basalt reliefs — many of them to be seen at the museum. In the Holy of Holies at the heart of this temple, an altar for offering incense was found on which was carved a cross contained within a circle, symbol of Baal Hadad, the Canaanite storm god. As you leave, notice the elaborate nests which the swallows have built underneath the eaves of the museum and, on the left of the path, a drain from the eighteenth century B.C.

Afterwards, continue north on Route 90 until you reach a road to the right signposted the Huleh Nature Reserve. Before arriving at the entrance to the nature reserve, a road to the right is signposted Dubrovin's Farm.

Lunch at Dubrovin's Farm

The Dubrovin family came to the Huleh Valley from Russia in the 1890s, at a time when many Jewish immigrants were attempting to establish themselves in the Holy Land. The farm is now surrounded by orchards and rich agricultural land, but the Huleh Valley at that time was a mosquito-ridden swamp. Such terrain was acquired by the newcomers because it was malarial, unused by the Palestinian inhabitants. But the land frequently created great problems for the immigrants — most of them had come from the cities of Eastern Europe and knew nothing of farming. The Dubrovins were different. Surprisingly, they were not Jews but were sympathetic to Jewish aspirations. And they succeeded where others failed, because they came from a farming background. They knew how to drain and to cultivate this land.

Look around the farm yard, organized in a neat square, the buildings facing inwards. It is now a little agricultural museum — the farm implements used by the Dubrovins are on show. Notice particularly the threshing sledges — the people of the Old Testament used sledges like this. Pieces of flint were lodged in the holes, and a sledge was harnessed to an ox or a donkey. Then the farmer stood on the sledge and was pulled round and round through the stalks of wheat or barley, lacerating them ready for winnowing. A barn in the corner of this farmyard has been converted into a restaurant — the food is excellent, served with the freshest of all possible vegetables and fruit.

Return to the main road, and continue north on Route 90 for about twelve miles, then turn right onto Route 99. About six miles further on, the remains of ancient Dan lie down a road to the left.

Dan

The Old Testament on several occasions (Judges 20, 1 for instance) refers to the Holy Land as extending 'from Dan to Beersheba'. Tel Dan is a fairly large mound in a luxuriant nature reserve. The car park is southwest of the ancient site — you walk to the tel through the woods alongside the abundant flowing waters of the River Dan, fed by melting snows from the heights of Mount Hermon which hangs above the river valley. The springs which supply the river rise further north across the Lebanese border. This is the only part of the Holy Land which is not short of water. Tabor oaks, pistachio trees, Syrian ash, white poplars, mulberries and grapevines grow in profusion. Myrtle, buckthorn, laurel and St John's Wort abound.

Like Hazor, this was a great Bronze Age walled city — called Laish in the Canaanite period. The tel itself is also heavily wooded — tracks lead you through the trees in the direction of the various archaeological sites on the tel. Skirt the mound on the southern side. Continuous occupation over a very long period has made investigation of the tel a complex task. But you can see the remains of the thick basalt walls which constituted the defences of the city. Continue along this path to the eastern side of the mound. Here you will find one of the treasures of ancient Dan.

An arched gateway, in remarkably good condition, built of mudbrick in the Canaanite period has been excavated on the edge of the tel. It illustrates the sophistication of the Canaanite fortifications. The road up to the gate curved from the left, ensuring that troops approaching the city would expose their unprotected right sides to the defenders — shields were carried on the left arm. Three wooden doors and two guard rooms were incorporated into the gateway.

Amphorae, juglets, flasks, bronze bowls, oil lamps, swords, ivory cosmetic boxes, and much gold and silver jewellery were discovered during the excavations of Dan — exactly as might be expected of a trading city built on the Way of the Sea. Many of these artifacts are now to be seen in the Israel Museum, Jerusalem. The city was taken by the Israelite tribe called Dan, probably in the twelfth century B.C.

... the Danites came to Laish, to a people quiet and unsuspecting, and smote them with the edge of the sword, and burned the city with fire ... And they named the city Dan, after the name of Dan their ancestor ...

The Danites had originally settled in the foothills near the Plain of Sharon, but had come into conflict with the Philistines who arrived in the coastal plain at about the same time. It explains the migration of the tribe to the Upper Jordan Valley — behaviour much disapproved of by the biblical writers.

During the Israelite period, Dan was recognized as one of the sacred cities of Israel. Jeroboam, son of Nebat, the first king of the northern kingdom, set up a golden calf in a sanctuary at Dan.

The tel at Dan is one of the most attractive sites in the countryside. The ancient city was abandoned in Old Testament times and has never been reoccupied. But now the tel, surrounded by luxuriant woodlands and rich agricultural land, is a tourist attraction, a haven of wild birds and flowers.

After leaving Dan, continue along Route 99 to Banias. Notice the massive block of Mount Hermon on the left — snow-covered for most of the year. The base of the valley is flat, heavily wooded in places. As the modern road begins to rise towards the Golan Heights, the road twists and turns. On the left is the wooded valley where lies the site of Banias — like Dan a tourist attraction and an archaeological site.

Banias

In ancient times, the river Hermon spilled over from a deep pool within a cave at Banias, forming a wide stream. The phenomenon was miraculous, puzzling the ancients. They believed the pool was fed with water from a lake called Phiale higher up on the Golan Heights. The original name Panias reflects the world of the Greeks — people believed that the nature god Pan and his nymphs danced through these forests. Niches from the Graeco-Roman period can still be seen cut into the rocks above the river. One bears an inscription to Pan and was evidently meant to contain his statue; the rest were for his retinue of nymphs.

But the stream no longer comes from a cave. Instead, waters burst everywhere out of the rocks below. They come through the porous rocks of Mount Hermon from the melting snows above. A town first appears in the history books here with the Seleucid victory over the Ptolemies in 198 B.C. Mark Antony gave Panias to Cleopatra. Later, Herod the Great received it from Caesar Augustus. Herod built a white marble temple here, dedicated to the emperor. After Herod's death, Philip rebuilt the town, naming it Caesarea — it was known as Caesarea Philippi to differentiate the place from Caesarea Maritima.

The New Testament tells us that Jesus and his disciples make a journey through the Upper Jordan Valley to visit Caesarea Philippi. Here, within the context of a pagan shrine, Peter describes Jesus as 'The Christ', and in return Peter is called 'the rock on which I will build my church'. Later, Jesus together with his closest disciples, Peter, James and John, go for a long hill walk from Caesarea Philippi — very likely in the foothills of Mount Hermon. During that walk, they received the vision in which Jesus was transfigured and was in the company of Moses and Elijah. Today, the town is relatively small, a popular place for tourists and pilgrims. There is a car park at the entrance to the site. Head first for the stream, then cross where it emerges out of the rocks to see the niches dedicated to Pan and his nymphs. Notice the Greek inscriptions alongside the niches. Afterwards follow the river down to stroll along the banks, a haven of water and bird life.

Leaving Banias, continue on Route 99 for about five miles before turning right onto a regional road 978 which will take you across the Golan Heights.

The Golan Heights

At first the road runs through the rugged foothills south of Mount Hermon. But soon the Golan Heights proper emerge, a wide open prairie orientated gently towards Damascus. This is part of the territories occupied by Israel since the Six Day War of 1967, but in character the land belongs to Syria rather than to the Holy Land. The Holy Land, in general, is sheep and goat country — this is cattle country. Since the earliest times, the Golan Heights have been occupied by a cosmopolitan mixture of peoples.

About thirteen miles further on, go right onto Route 91, then after about five miles turn left. After about four miles, turn left again and then a mile further on turn right along a regional road. About six miles along this road there is a turning to the right signposted Gamla. As you drive along this road in the direction of the Jordan valley, notice the dolmens and the remains of shaft tombs built of basalt by the nomadic peoples of the Golan in the Middle Bronze period.

Gamla

Leave your car in the car park for Gamla, about half a mile from the archaeological site. There are no modern buildings but you are likely to encounter coachloads of tourists visiting the site. It is very popular with Israelis in particular.

You approach the remains of the ancient city on a rough track from the east. One glimpse of the site is enough to explain why this city was called 'camel'. The high mountain crest on which the city was built is shaped exactly like a camel's back. Gamla is first mentioned among the cities conquered by Alexander Janneus early in the first century B.C. But the most dramatic episode in the history of this city came during the campaign of the Roman general Vespasian to retake the Holy Land after the Jewish revolt of A.D. 66.

The initial stages of the Roman campaign were in Galilee where Joseph ben Matthias was commander of the Jewish forces. The Romans played cat and mouse with Matthias, finally trapping him at Jotapata north of Nazareth. The Jewish zealots hid themselves in a cave beneath the city and made a suicide pact. As the Romans broke in, each man killed his neighbour. But when it came to Matthias who was expected to die last, he decided instead to join the Romans. Afterwards, he became firm friends with Vespasian, and changed his name to Josephus Flavius. When Vespasian became Emperor, he took Josephus to Rome and made him an imperial pensioner. Josephus was a traitor. Yet we are greatly indebted to him. Little would be known of Jewish history, particularly in the Roman period, were it not for the books which he wrote. He was an eyewitness to the siege of Gamla in A.D. 67 and described it in *The Jewish War*.

The Romans began by establishing themselves on the high ground east of the ridge. The highest tower of the defences of Gamla confronted them, and a trench had been dug across their line of attack. The city, as Josephus describes it, was a remarkable sight:

> The houses were built against the steep mountain flank and were astonishingly huddled together, one over the other; as a result of its steepness the town

seemed to hang in the air and looked as if it were about to topple headlong upon itself. It faced south, and its southern crest, which rose to an immense height, formed the citadel; below this an unwalled precipice fell away to the ravines.

Being one of the last cities in Galilee to come under Roman attack, Gamla was packed with refugees.

At first the Jews were able to beat back the Roman forces as they tried to bring up equipment to attack the city walls. The defenders were eventually forced to withdraw, driven back by stones from catapults and slings. The walls were attacked with battering rams, and the Romans swarmed into the city. But the Jews took advantage of the high ground around the crest to harass the enemy trapped below them in the narrow lanes of the city. Many of the Romans climbed onto the roofs of the houses which collapsed under their weight, houses then falling onto other houses on the steep slope. The situation was chaotic — falling masonry, trapped Roman soldiers, panic-stricken Jewish families. The Romans who survived were forced to withdraw.

It took the Romans a long time to capture Gamla. The city was finally taken during a storm, and Josephus tells us that during the ferocious battle over five thousand Jews, men, women and children, met their deaths by falling down the steep mountain side into the ravine. As you approach the ridge on which Gamla stood, you will see on a plaque in the rocks Josephus's exciting description of the siege. To read it aloud while looking at the scene of the battle brings it all to life. Josephus was certainly a reliable reporter of events — except, of course, when he himself was involved in the action.

While much of the Golan is very fertile, the region where the high lands give way to the Jordan rift is rough land, largely uncultivated. Below, however, can be seen the rich fields verging on the Sea of Galilee.

After Gamla continue on the regional road 869 down to the Sea of Galilee. You can return to Tiberias either by taking Route 92 around the southern end of the lake (the long route) or follow the lakeside road north.

Overnight at Tiberias.

For restaurants and accommodation in Tiberias, see p. 88-9.

Dubrovin's Farm can be found adjoining the Huleh Valley Nature Reserve —
it is signposted on Route 90.

DAN: USEFUL INFORMATION

Government Tourist Information Office, Town Hall,
Safed (tel: 067-30633)

Facilities:	archaeological site, there is an interesting nature trail through the Dan nature reserve

---

BANIAS: USEFUL INFORMATION

Population:	5,000
Altitude:	sea level
Facilities:	riverside walks, shrine to the god Pan

Tiberias 44 miles

DAY 7

Tiberias, Nazareth, Akko and Tel Aviv: approximately 120 miles

Leave Tiberias and head first to Nazareth where Jesus grew up. To the south lies the extensive table land of the Valley of Jezreel. Perhaps cross Jezreel to Megiddo, the biblical Armageddon, at the head of Iron Pass through the Carmel Range. Then investigate the mediaeval city at Akko, the Acre of the Crusaders — few cities can boast so long or so eventful a history. Afterwards, drive south along the coastal highway to spend a night out in Tel Aviv.

Map references
Nazareth   178:234
Akko   158:258
Megiddo   167:221
Tel Aviv   130:165

Route shown p. 112.

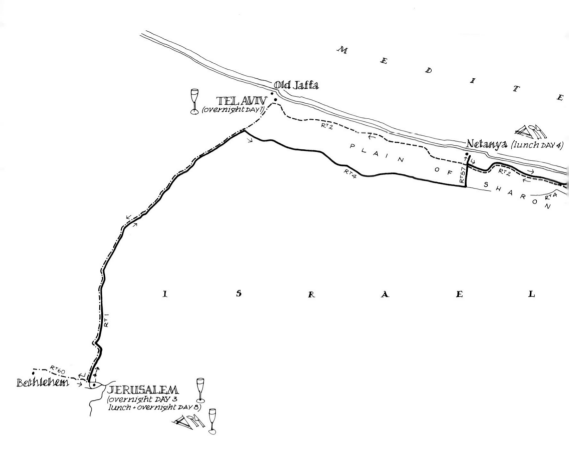

Begin by taking a last look at the Sea of Galilee — you will not see this magical and evocative lake again in these travels. Then from Tiberias follow Route 77 which snakes to the west out of the rift valley.

Detour

On your right about seven miles out of Tiberias is a curiously-shaped hill called the Horns of Hittim. A footpath leads from the main road to the top of the hill — about half an hour's walk. This was the scene of the Sultan Saladin's crucial battle with the Crusaders in 1187.

The Muslim army had crossed the Jordan south of the Sea of Galilee and was encamped near the river. The Crusaders had mobilized about 20,000 men against them, including 1,200 cavalry, and were stationed at Zippori northwest of Nazareth. Saladin's first move was to blockade Tiberias. On 3rd July 1187, the hottest day of the year, King Guy of Lusignan ordered the Crusader army to advance. During that long day's march on Tiberias, the knights, constantly harassed by the enemy, were roasted in their armour. They spent a terrible night without water while the enemy lit grass fires around them. On 4th July, they engaged the Muslim forces in fierce combat on the Horns of Hittim. Saladin's final charge on that day effectively put an end to Crusader dominance of the Holy Land. Jerusalem fell to him soon after, and from thenceforth the Crusader activity was largely confined to the Mediterranean coast around Akko — then called Acre.

About twelve miles from Tiberias turn left onto Route 75 for Nazareth. About a mile further on, the road passes through a village called Kafr Kanna — wrongly identified with the biblical Cana of Galilee where Jesus turned water into wine at a wedding. A small Greek Orthodox Church up a side street to the right commemorates the miracle. Interestingly, St Jerome visited this village believing it to be Cana when he made his pilgrimage through the Holy Land at the end of the fourth century. The real Cana is an unexcavated tel, north of Nazareth, in an inaccessible valley in the Beth Netofa Range. To get there from Nazareth means crossing the marshy Beth Netofa Valley, flooded in the winter months. As early as the fourth century, the tour operators had for convenience re-sited Cana.

Nazareth

Nazareth is not mentioned in the Old Testament, and became important only because Jesus was brought up here. In his time this was a small ancient village off the beaten track, occupying a basin in the hills north of the Valley of Jezreel. Yet there were many contacts with the outside world. People used to say that while a Judean road ran nowhere, Galilean roads ran everywhere. Certainly, the Way of the Sea in the Valley of Jezreel south of the village ran to Damascus in the north and to the port at Caesarea Maritima in the south. The New Testament tells of a village excursion to Jerusalem for the feast of the Passover when Jesus was twelve. Jesus lived in the village until he was about thirty years old. He then went to the Jordan valley near Jericho to be baptised by John the Baptist. Afterwards, he settled at Capernaum where he began his ministry. When he did return to the village, he caused an uproar at the synagogue with his claims of messiahship.

Nazareth today is an extensive town in which Arab Christians form the majority of the population. Two large Roman Catholic churches in the centre of the town are worth visiting — the Church of the Annunciation and the Church of St Joseph. The Church of the Annunciation is believed to be on the site of Mary's home, where she experienced the visitation of the Angel Gabriel. The Church of St Joseph is believed to be sited where the holy family lived and where Joseph had his carpenter's workshop.

These two sites have been venerated since early in the Christian tradition. In the centuries following the birth of Christianity, Nazareth became a centre of the Judaeo-Christians. There was disagreement between the Christians who wished to observe all the Jewish laws and those, like St Paul, who saw the new religion as having a separate identity. The Church eventually decided that the Jewish laws were unnecessary for Christians, but the Judaeo-Christians continued to observe them. Evidence of their ideas can be found in the crypt under the Church of St Joseph. The remains of a baptismal font from that period could also be used as a Jewish ritual bath. The Judaeo-Christians divided themselves into a number of different sects early in their history. Those at Nazareth belonged to a sect called the Nazarenes. Some of their leaders claimed kinship with Jesus himself.

The magnificent Church of the Annunciation at Nazareth was consecrated in 1969, the work of the Italian architect Giovanni Muzio. Panels from around the world reflect the universal nature of the Church, and many fine works of art have been incorporated within its walls. But this is the fifth church to be built on this site, and structures from each of the earlier churches have been retained within it. The Grotto of the Annunciation in the basement of the building dates back to the Byzantine period. Outside the church, excavations from the time of Jesus reveal grain silos and the remains of primitive buildings.

Detour

Leave Nazareth in your car on Route 60 and descend south into the table-land plain of the Valley of Jezreel, a vast patchwork of large open fields in which a great variety of different crops are grown — wheat, barley, tobacco and cotton. The sides of the surrounding mountains are well wooded with olive and almond trees. Nearly all the ancient settlements were built on higher ground above the base of the valley. It was important that they should be defensible in time of war. At Afula, turn right onto Route 65, the line in ancient times of the Way of the Sea. It leads to Megiddo at the head of Iron Pass.

Megiddo

There is a good restaurant at the entrance to the archaeological site at Megiddo, eminently suitable for a midday meal. Before climbing the tel, it is also worth visiting the small museum nearby if only to study the excellent model of Megiddo in the eighth century B.C. This is one of the most important of all the city mounds in the Holy Land — not even Jericho has been so extensively investigated. For over two thousand five hundred years, Megiddo was the city-fortress which controlled the entrance to the Valley of Jezreel from the south, the almost invariable route of warring armies between the centres of power in the Nile valley on the one side and the valley of the Tigris and Euphrates on the other. The city was destroyed and rebuilt again and again — this is not one city, but twenty-five cities each superimposed on the last. It explains why this site is extremely confusing to the visitor.

The photographs at the museum are also worth studying. A great palace was built at Megiddo during the Canaanite period and was in use for several centuries. Rich hoards of jewellery and ivories have been recovered from this palace, affording considerable insights into Canaanite art and culture. Ivories inlaid in pieces of furniture at the palace are one example of how Canaanite Megiddo reflected cosmopolitan tastes derived from the many contacts provided by the Way of the Sea.

On leaving the museum, climb the tel and take the first path to the left. You will see where the archaeologists have excavated down to near bedrock level. From the earliest times, this was the religious centre of the city. A round Canaanite

Ivory depicting a Canaanite king celebrating a victory — found at Megiddo

altar, built of small rubble stones, has been excavated at this level — it is one of the most easily recognisable features of the site. The first settlement came into existence near a spring which flowed out of a cave sometime in the fourth millennium B.C. By 3000 BC., Megiddo was a powerful city surrounded by massive mudbrick walls. Temples and other public buildings had been built. Although the altar is not Israelite, it conforms to the biblical instructions about such altars.

> And if you make me an altar of stone, you shall not build it of hewn stones; for if you wield your tool upon it you profane it.

The numerous bones found in the vicinity of this altar prove that sacrifices were made here.

The king of Megiddo is listed as one of the Canaanite rulers defeated by the Israelites during Joshua's military campaign in the mid-twelfth century B.C. But the Bible does not say that the city was taken — indeed, the Old Testament complains that the tribe of Manasseh failed to capture Megiddo. Probably, the city did not come into Israelite hands until the reign of King David. In the tenth century B.C. Solomon used forced labour to refortify the city. Later, Omri, king of Israel, and his son Ahab carried out extensive building works at Megiddo.

Go to the western side of the tel to see the water system. A small shaft to bring water into the city had been dug in the time of Solomon. But, as at Hazor, a major water shaft was eventually made. A vertical shaft was sunk through the mound — faced with stone where it passed through the debris of previous generations. Then a horizontal tunnel leading to the spring was cut through the bedrock.

At the apex of the mound, you can see the substantial grain silo at Megiddo constructed in the reign of Jeroboam II in the eighth century B.C. Steps running down into the base of the silo meant that grain could be collected from the level of the stores at any given time. The size of the silo reflects the fertility of the Valley of Jezreel.

The end of Megiddo came in 609 B.C. when Necho, the Egyptian Pharoah, made a military expedition to the Mesopotamian Valley. Josiah, king of Judah, confronted the Egyptians near Megiddo — the plan, no doubt, was to catch them in the Iron Pass. But the Jewish army was defeated and the king was killed. Afterwards, the role of guarding the Iron Pass fell to the small village of Kefar Otnay — eventually to become the base of the Roman Sixth Legion. Megiddo's strategic importance was over, but it was remembered centuries later when, in the New Testament, the final battle at the end of days was set at Armageddon. It is now a major archaeological site in the Holy Land.

Afterwards, to visit Akko, take Route 66 for Haifa and the coastal highway.

For those preferring not to visit Megiddo, take Route 79 out of Nazareth and pass through the undulating hills of the Shephelah of Galilee. After about twelve miles, turn right onto Route 70 which skirts the boundaries of the coastal plain of Akko. Ten miles further on turn left onto Route 85 for Akko itself.

Akko

To establish a port for the Holy Land was difficult in ancient times because irregular reefs of basalt run the whole length of this coastline just off the shore — the problem encountered by Herod the Great when he built Caesarea Maritima. With the exception of Akko and, further north, Tyre, nothing remotely resembling a natural harbour exists on this coast. It explains why Akko, on a small promontory on the Bay of Haifa, was the principal port of the Holy Land in ancient times. Yet the original city was not built on the coast. The tel stands alongside Route 85, on the outskirts of the modern town about three quarters of a mile inland — perhaps built there to protect it from invaders from the sea. The steep-sided tel rises to a height of about eighty feet. You can make a brief stop at the tel on the way into the town.

There is relatively little to see at the tel. The excavations have revealed the remains of a gateway built in mud brick — from about the same period as the Canaanite gateway at Dan but in nothing like as good a condition. On the north side of the mound, the archaeologists have cut a deep section into the tel, illustrating the strata at different periods. Yet in its day, this was a very important city. A branch of the Way of the Sea passed this way to Megiddo and the south. Another route led eastwards through the Turan Valley to the Sea of Galilee. And a tortuous road led through the hills of Upper Galilee to Dan in the north. The Phoenicians who controlled this coastal city were much involved with trade by sea, and there is evidence that the pottery and artifacts which passed through the port travelled long distances in early times.

Leaving the tel drive into the Old City of Akko, a little inland from the port. The tel was abandoned in the sixth century B.C. when the centre of activity moved towards the port. The present buildings are mostly Crusader or Turkish, but this site has been occupied since the sixth century B.C. — a place of markets and camel trains. In the Hellenistic period the city was renamed Ptolemais in honour of Ptolemy, ruler of Egypt. It was still called Ptolemais in A.D. 53 when St Paul arrived at the end of his third missionary journey. In 68, the Roman general Vespasian made the city his military base for the suppression of the Jewish revolt in Galilee. The economy of Ptolemais boomed in the Byzantine period. The city surrendered to the Arabs in A.D. 636, and resumed its original name.

Akko was taken by the Crusaders in 1104. It was re-captured by Saladin in 1187 after his victory on the Horns of Hittim, and was retaken by Richard Coeur de Lion and Philip Augustus in 1191. The Crusaders renamed the city St Jean d'Acre. From then on, it was the capital of the Latin kingdom. Fleets from Genoa, Venice and other Italian ports supplied Acre, and there were colonies of Italians in the city. The Knights Hospitalers, the Templars, the Teutonic Knights and the Order of St Lazarus all had their quarters here.

In 1291, the complete destruction of Acre by the Mamelukes marked the end of the Crusader kingdom. For over three hundred years the port and the city were left in ruins. But in the seventeenth century the Druze Emir Fakhr e-Din rebuilt part of the city, and the work was continued in the eighteenth century. Most notable of the builders was Ahmad el-Jazzar who ruled 1775-1804. He was the Ottoman governor of Sidon, a man of legendary cruelty — it was said that he had his workers buried alive and murdered his wives with his bare hands. With the help of the British fleet, he successfully defended Akko against Napoleon in 1799.

The Old City presents the visitor with a fascinating mixture of styles, Crusader and Turkish, dominated by the beautiful, green-domed El-Jazzar mosque. There are excellent restaurants here, and a great variety of shops. It is worth visiting the El-Jazzar mosque first notice the tranquil courtyard and the fine mosaics. On the other side of the street is the entrance to the massive complex of Crusader buildings — the El-Jazzar mosque was built on top of the Crusader remains filled with earth and stone. They have now been excavated, and it is possible to wander through the great halls of Crusader Acre which were buried for centuries.

Afterwards, wander through the streets of the Old City down to the port itself

— nowadays a haven for small craft. There are few places in the Holy Land with more character. Notice the high-walled houses, complete with balconies, overlooking the streets. Here and there are the arched remains of lock-up shops, and tall Greek-style towers of churches-turned-mosques. Some of the buildings, too, have been decorated by graffiti artists.

Follow Route 4 to the northernmost point of the plain of Akko where the mountains of Upper Galilee run down at a steep angle into the sea. It is one of the most beautiful places in all the Holy Land. White cliffs descend into the waters, it is called the Ladder of Tyre. The black basalt rocks at shore level just south of the cliffs impede the flow of the waves so that great sprays kick up, then fall frothing and bubbling. In ancient times, these mountains impeded invading forces from the north. To 'climb the Ladder of Tyre' was to lay open the coastal plains of the south. It was achieved by many invading forces. Alexander the Great, for instance, took the city of Tyre on the island off the coast to the north in 332 B.C. after the longest and bloodiest siege of all his campaigns. It was his greatest military achievement. Then his forces crossed the Ladder of Tyre and, within a very short time, were in Gaza.

Afterwards, take the coastal highway, Route 4 to Haifa — the modern streets are forced down to the water's edge and the port by the Carmel promontory which descends here to the sea. This is a city of heavy industry, shipping and warehouses — although high above on the promontory itself can be seen the high-rise block of Haifa University. From thence by Route 2 to Tel Aviv.

Tel Aviv is the liveliest city in the Holy Land when it comes to night life. The hotels along the water front all have bars, discos and night clubs. Dizengoff Street, parallel to the sea, is the smart part of Tel Aviv — a world of boutiques, restaurants and space-age Israeli architecture. Elsewhere the city sprawls in a thousand suburbs. To the south is Old Jaffa, the Joppa of the New Testament. The little port is surrounded by smart shops and restaurants.

Overnight at Tel Aviv.

Rock-cut tomb in the Kidron Valley, Jerusalem

A Selection of Tel Aviv Hotels

Dan Arcadia, five star, out of town at Herzlia (tel: 052-556677)

Hilton, five star, Independence Park (tel: 244222)

Sheraton, five star, 115 Hayarkon Street (tel: 286222)

Ramada Continental, five star, 121Hayarkon Street (tel: 296444)

Sinai Hotel, five star, 11 Trumpeldor Street (tel: 652621)

Adiv, four star, 2 Mendele Street (tel: 229141)

Habakuk, four star, 7 Habakuk Street (tel: 440011)

Dizengoff Square, three star, 2 Zamenhof Street (tel: 296181)

Florida, three star, 164 Hayarkon Street (tel: 242184)

Restaurants in Tel Aviv

For an expensive meal, the **Sheraton Hotel** (tel: 286222) has an excellent fish restaurant.

Tzamaret Aviv, 43 Brodetzky Street (tel: 410678)

Keton, 145 Dizengoff Street (tel: 233697) — Eastern European cuisine

Yin Yang 64 Rothschild Boulevard (tel: 621833) — good Chinese

Banana, 334 Dizengoff Street (tel: 457491) — vegetarian cuisine

Entertainment

The Bell at the north end of Ben Yehuda Street, good for jazz.

Or take a taxi to Old Jaffa, full of places for food and entertainment.

Restaurants in Old Jaffa
Alhambra, 30 Jerusalem Boulevard, Jaffa (tel: 834453)

Entertainment
The Cave, Kedumim Square, Old Jaffa for Israeli folk music

The Younes Restaurant in Old Jaffa specializes in Arab fish foods, shishkebabs and salads

---

NAZARETH: USEFUL INFORMATION

Government Tourist Information Office: Casanova Street (tel: 70555)

Population:	39,000
Altitude:	1,200 ft
Facilities:	churches, restaurants, markets

Akko 28 miles

AKKO: USEFUL INFORMATION

Government Tourist Information Office: Town Hall, Weizmann Street (tel: 910251)

Population:	36,800
Altitude:	66 ft
Facilities:	hotels, restaurants, beaches, archaeological sites, mediaeval city

Tel Aviv 73 miles

TEL AVIV: USEFUL INFORMATION

Government Tourist Information Office: 7 Mendele
Street (tel: 223266)

Population:	353,000
Altitude:	sea level
Facilities:	museums, hotels, restaurants, discos, night clubs, beaches, theatre, opera, concerts

Jerusalem 40 miles

The Souk in the old city, Jerusalem

DAY 8

Tel Aviv, Bethlehem, in and around Jerusalem: approximately 50 miles

Leaving Tel Aviv head first for Bethlehem, via Jerusalem. See the Church of the Nativity built by Constantine the Great over the cave where it was believed Jesus was born. Return to Jerusalem and visit the grounds of the Hotel Holyland where an accurate model has been built of Jerusalem in the first century. Afterwards, ascend the Mount of Olives to see the Old City of today, the Chapel of the Ascension and the Pater Noster Convent. Descend into the deep Valley of the Kidron to visit the site of the Garden of Gesthemane, and see the ancient rock-hewn tombs which Jesus saw in his time. Then visit the Rockerfeller Museum and the Israel Museum to see treasures, many of them discovered in places already visited during these travels.

Map reference
Bethlehem 169:123

Route shown p. 112

Breakfast at Tel Aviv.

Leave Tel Aviv towards Jerusalem on Route 1. Passing through Jerusalem take Route 60 south to Bethlehem.

Bethlehem

This is now a large Arab township quite unlike the 'little town of Bethlehem' celebrated in the Christmas carol. Manger Square, which faces the Church of the Nativity, is a vortex of bustling humanity, busy restaurants, souvenir shops and snarled-up traffic. In the back streets, small factories are turning out endless camels, donkeys and Nativity sets in olive wood to sell to the tourists. Yet the brindled slopes of the Judean hill country look much the same today as they did when Mary and Joseph came to the city before the birth of their child, and the terracing which supports the vines and olive trees around Bethlehem dates back to Old Testament times. Nor is the city simply to be associated with the birth of Christ. Bethlehem is also remembered for the marriage of Ruth and Boaz, and was the childhood home of David, the greatest of all the kings of Israel. At the end of the fourth century St Jerome translated the Bible at Bethlehem from the original Hebrew and Greek into the Latin of the Vulgate, the 'book of the people'.

Visit the Church of the Nativity, first built early in the fourth century by Constantine the Great, the first Christian emperor of Rome. This church is often described as the work of Helena, Constantine's mother, but it seems unlikely. Contemporary records tell us very little about Constantine's building, but the general pattern of it has emerged as a result of the work of the archaeologists. Strikingly, it is very similar in plan to the original Church of the Holy Sepulchre. It seems that just as a rock-cut tomb was found at Jerusalem to identify the place of Jesus' burial, so was a cave discovered at Bethlehem in which to place Jesus' birth. The gospels do not say that Jesus was born in a cave, but Justin Martyr writing in about A.D. 150 says that Mary bore Christ in a cave 'very near to Bethlehem'. The present basilica is the result of a sixth-century rebuilding of the church by Justinian and the Crusader repairs of the twelfth century, although trapdoors in the floor reveal the mosaic of Constantine's building.

This church survived the Persian invasion of the Holy Land in the seventh century — some say because a contemporary painting depicted the Wise Men from the East dressed in Persian attire. The wooden ceiling is of English oak, a gift of King Edward IV in the fifteenth century. The cave, identified by Constantine as the birthplace of Christ, lies underneath the high altar of the church and is reached by stairways from either side. A silver star marks the supposed birthplace. Next to it, the Chapel of the Manger is the place where it is believed Mary placed her newborn son. As with the Via Dolorosa (p. 63-4) there is no real evidence for believing that this really was the place. But the Church of the Nativity remains a useful site for the contemplation of the mysteries of the birth of Christ.

Lunch at Jerusalem.

Return to Jerusalem on Route 60. On entering Jerusalem, go left into King David Street, then left again on Jabotinsky Street. Take one of the turnings to the right to bring you into Gereck Aza — the traditional Gaza Road. Fork right into Rav Herzog and follow this street until you come to the entrance to the grounds of the Holyland Hotel on your right. The model of first-century Jerusalem, continuously updated by the archaeologists as they make new discoveries, is owned by the hotel and is set in these lovely grounds. This is also, perhaps, an opportunity for lunch at the hotel.

Jerusalem in the first century

Before studying the model, look again at the plan of Jerusalem in Jesus' time on page 59. The biblical city was destroyed by the Romans after the suppression of the Bar Cochba revolt in A.D. 135 — the Old City of today is largely the work of the Roman town planners who built Aelia Capitolina further up the ridges on which the city stood. The model, on a scale 1-50, helps the visitor to visualize the city as it was on the eve of the Jewish revolt in A.D. 66. Notice the Temple, the focal point of this city, built on a great platform and surrounded by courts, protected by the Antonia fortress in the northwest corner.

Opposite the Temple platform on the western side of the city stood the luxurious palace of King Herod the Great, used in Jesus' time as the Jerusalem residence of the Roman prefect. The northern end of the palace was protected by three towers called Hippicus, Mariamme and Phasael — named after Herod's brother, his favourite wife (whom he murdered) and his best friend. When the Romans destroyed this palace, they spared Phasael because they said it was so beautiful — it now forms the base of one of the towers in the Citadel near the Jaffa Gate. Notice the public auditorium at Herod's palace — almost certainly where Jesus was tried and condemned before Pontius Pilate. It was usual for Roman trials to be held in public, the proceedings influenced by opinions expressed by the crowd — precisely as the gospels describe. From there he was taken to Golgotha, the place of execution outside the northern wall of the city. There are many other fascinating aspects to this model — recorded explanations are available in several languages at various points around it.

Drive to Derech Aza Street and follow it through until you come to the western side of the Old City. Turn right and skirt the city wall all the way round until you come to the eastern side of the Old City. Turn right and descend into the Valley of the Kidron, then climb the hill opposite to the Mount of Olives. There is plenty of parking space on the long road which runs along the top of the Mount of Olives parallel to the wall of the Old City opposite.

The Mount of Olives

There is no better vantage point than this from which to view the Old City of Jerusalem. Jesus himself saw the city from here. Galilean Jews in his time did not travel south through the Samaritan hill country when they came to Jerusalem, because there was enmity between the Jews and the Samaritans. Instead, they crossed the Jordan south of the Sea of Galilee, and travelled on the other side of the river until they came to Jericho. They then approached the holy city from the east, and Jerusalem was revealed in all its glory as they came over the Mount of Olives. The most memorable of Jesus' arrivals at the city from the Mount of Olives was when he rode into Jerusalem on a donkey, surrounded by rejoicing crowds — remembered by the churches on Palm Sunday. Surprisingly, perhaps, the gospels give no indication that his entry into Jerusalem took him down into the deep ravine of the Kidron and up the other side.

But this is not the Jerusalem of Jesus' time — compare and contrast what you see with the model in the grounds of the Holyland Hotel. The original city of David was built on the ridge below the Temple platform, now almost entirely given over to archaeological excavations as the remains of the oldest part of the biblical city are investigated — the Jerusalem captured by King David from the Jebusites in the eleventh century B.C. To the north are the remains of the great platform constructed by Herod the Great as the base for the Temple

— nowadays occupied by the silver-domed El Aqsa Mosque and the magnificent shrine of the Dome of the Rock. The view of the platform from the Mount of Olives emphasizes the sheer scale of Herod's achievement — it defies the photographer even with a wide-angled lens. In a central position on this eastern side of the platform is the walled-in Golden Gate — there is an ancient belief that when the Golden Gate is opened the Messiah will come in all his glory.

The view from the Mount of Olives also affords the visitor the best view of the Old City of today, now a great forest of television aerials amid the domes and minarets. But it would be a mistake to leave this vantage point without also looking east from the Mount of Olives. Climb to the brow of the hill between the buildings. Away to the east lie the vast tracts of the Judean wilderness, austere and beautiful in the torrid heat. They emphasize the point that Jerusalem stands on the watershed of the Holy Land. To the west the land is green, but the desert also starts here.

The Mount of Olives is also associated with the Ascension of Jesus into heaven — it is commemorated by the remains of a Crusader chapel and, to the north, by the Russian Orthodox Church of the Ascension. A Byzantine church was built in the fourth century on the site of the present Crusader building — around the rock on which it was believed Jesus had stood to be taken into heaven. It was destroyed in the tenth century and replaced in the twelfth century by an octagonal church surrounded by fortifications — built to overlook the road from Jerusalem to Jericho. The church was destroyed at the end of the Crusader period, but the small chapel over the rock itself remains. Notice the ornate capitals to the columns. According to the Russian traditions, Jesus' ascension took place where the tower of their church now stands. But a much more elaborate Russian Orthodox church can be seen on the western slope of the Mount of Olives, built in the nineteenth century by Czar Alexander III, but in the seventeenth-century Russian style, a maze of onion-shaped gilded domes. The Pater Noster Convent is also interesting. This was the site of Constantine's great church on the Mount of Olives called Eleona. Copies of the Lord's Prayer in sixty languages can be seen on plaques in the cloisters of the convent, originally this was the crypt of Constantine's church.

The Garden of Gesthemane

In many ways, the fashion started by Constantine at the beginning of the fourth century of building churches on supposed holy sites can be counter-productive:

> 'Master,' said Peter, 'it is well we are here. Let us make three booths, one for you and one for Moses and one for Elijah.'

This was at the Transfiguration, when Jesus and his closest disciples had a vision in which they encountered Moses and Elijah. The folly of trying to perpetuate an experience with a building was certainly borne in on Peter. Yet Christians in particular have continued ever since to build churches in the Holy Land. Descend to the Church of the Agony at the base of the Valley of the Kidron, the supposed site of Jesus' arrest in the Garden of Gesthemane. The building, like that of the Church of the Beatitudes above the Sea of Galilee, is the work of the Italian architect Barlozzi. It is sometimes called the Church of All Nations because contributions were received from all over the world to pay for it. It was completed in 1924, and stands on the site of a Byzantine church — mosaics from the ancient church are incorporated into the floor of the present building. The most striking characteristic of this building is the splendid mosaic facade, depicting Christ as a link between God and man.

Nobody knows, of course, where the Garden of Gesthemane really was — the name means 'olive press' and there are certainly ancient olive trees and olive presses in the vicinity of the church. Afterwards, continue south on a small road which leads deeper into the Valley of the Kidron. This is the necropolis of ancient Jerusalem — a world of graves from many different periods. Notice in particular the large rock-cut tombs on the side of the valley — they were here when Jesus of Nazareth passed this way. Nobody knows who was buried in these tombs — they were made for wealthy citizens of Jerusalem in the Hellenistic period.

The remains of biblical Jerusalem

Look up from the base of the Valley of the Kidron at the southeastern corner of the Temple platform. Almost certainly, the pinnacle of the Temple, made famous in Jesus' temptations, stood on that corner dominating the scene. Then look at the ridge running south from the Temple platform — where the original city of David was built. The Millo, the central fortress of the city, stood on the apex of the ridge. From there David saw the beautiful Bathsheeba, wife of Uriah the Hittite, bathing on the rooftop of her house in Silwan, the village opposite.

The ancient water shaft cut through the rock to bring water into the city from the Gihon has recently been re-excavated — it was discovered by Warren in the 1860s and absent-mindedly filled in by later archaeologists. Further south, near a primary school, you will find further evidence of elaborate schemes to supply biblical Jerusalem with water. The entrance to Hezekiah's Tunnel lies beyond the school on the right-hand side of the road. For a small fee, you will be allowed through the gate to inspect the tunnel itself where, most of the year, a lively flow of water runs underneath the ridge to the Pool of Siloam. This shaft was cut in the eighth century B.C. during the reign of Hezekiah, king of Judah.

Return to the main road towards Jerusalem from the Valley of the Kidron, and drive westwards round the perimeter of the Old City. As you come to the west side, you will see the King David Hotel overlooking the valley. Take the road Derech Hebron to the left, past Montefiori's Windmill, and enter King David Street. On the right of the hotel is a little park overlooking the Old City.

Herod's family tomb

King Herod the Great died in 4 B.C., and was buried at his great palace fortress called Herodion, near Bethlehem. According to Josephus, a great treasure was buried with him, but his tomb has never been found. Herod's family tomb, however, is to be found in the little park just beside the King David Hotel.

The method of burial in the Holy Land from the last Canaanite period was in rock-cut tombs, many of them sealed with a circular stone fitted into a groove. The deceased was wrapped in a winding sheet and placed inside a chamber within the tomb — there were usually several chambers. The tomb was then sealed and left for twelve months to allow the body to decay. Eventually the tomb was re-opened and the bones of the deceased were placed in an ossuary, which was stored somewhere in the tomb. The tomb was then ready for re-use.

Detour

If you have time, the Rockerfeller Museum on Sultan Suleiman Street north of the Old City is worth a visit. In relation to these travels notice in particular the fine ossuaries, the ivories from Megiddo and Islamic carvings from the El Aqsa Mosque.

The board games found on the pavements of Capernaum (see p. 96) and in Jerusalem (see p. 64) are sometimes set up for people to play at the Museum.

Continue westwards to the Israel Museum on Rehavia Park. In the grounds is the magnificent Shrine of the Book, a modern building designed specifically to take the Dead Sea Scrolls and reflecting the scroll motif. The Isaiah scroll, first discovered by the bedouin smugglers in 1947, takes pride of place in the centre of the museum. Notice also other artifacts found at Qumran — particularly an ordinary looking glass dish. It would cost, it seems, a few pounds in the shops. But it is two thousand years old, in perfect condition and was found at Qumran. The museum proper contains a fascinating collection of artifacts from all over the Holy Land — it is also an art gallery. There is a good restaurant at the museum.

Afterwards, have a last look around the city before returning to your hotel.

Overnight in Jerusalem.

For details of accommodation, see pp 65-6.

Museums
Rockerfeller: open daily 10.00 a.m.-5.00 p.m., except Friday and Saturday when it is open until 2 p.m.

Israel Museum: open Sunday, Monday, Tuesday and Thursday 10.00 a.m.-5.00 p.m., Tuesday 4.00-10.00 p.m., Friday and Saturday 10.00 a.m.-2 p.m.

BETHLEHEM: USEFUL INFORMATION

Government Tourist Information Office: Manger Square (tel: 942591)

Population:	20,000
Altitude:	2,462 ft
Facilities:	churches, restaurants

Jerusalem 6 miles

DAY 9

Jerusalem, across the Jordan, the King's Highway, the Wadi Mujib, Kerak and Petra: approximately 180 miles

Leave Jerusalem early — aim to be over the bridge by mid-morning. Take the road to Madaba and follow the famous King's Highway south through the majestic Wadi Mujib. Lunch at the Rest House at Kerak and visit the Crusader castle, in its time the most sophisticated stronghold in the Middle East. See the spring where it is said that Moses brought water from the living rock, and arrive at Petra for a meal in the cool of the evening.

Map references
Kerak   227:66
Petra   192:971

Route shown p. 68.

Breakfast in Jerusalem.

Leave Jerusalem at about 6.30 a.m. The lorries exporting goods into Jordan and the tourist vehicles queue outside the military area at Jericho waiting for the bridge to open at 8 a.m. The procedure is virtually the reverse of the crossing of Day 2 (p. 56-7), although the formalities on the Jordanian side are not so stringent — all that is required is a valid passport not stamped by the Israelis and a copy of the document from the Ministry of Tourism at Amman. There is no bridge tax to pay on the Jordanian side.

While the use of a hire car or mini bus is a good idea in Israel and the West Bank territories, it is advisable on this part of the visit to Jordan in particular to use a taxi or a coach. Taxis or coaches *must* be booked at Amman beforehand — there are no facilities at the bridge for taking the visitor to Petra, or at Petra for getting visitors to the airport at the end of the itinerary. It is easy to get lost, the distances are considerable and the roads vary in quality.

On leaving the minor roads from the bridge, head for Amman. At Na'ur, turn right on the ancient King's Highway leading to Madaba. Then continue south. The road leads through the moon-like landscape of the rift valley, then rises towards the transjordanian plateau. It is hot, barren and, in its own way, quite beautiful. In the distance can still be seen the oasis at Jericho — the one patch of green in this desolate landscape.

Detour

Visit Machaerus, the remains of the great fortress of King Herod the Great east of the Dead Sea — the stronghold stood in the hills about thirteen miles west of the King's Highway. To get to Machaerus — now called Mukawir — turn right at the village called Libb about twenty-six miles south of Amman. Machaerus was Herod's formidable retreat in the hills east of the Jordan.

The flat-topped mountain spur on which Machaerus stood hangs high above deep wadis which descend to the Dead Sea. Unlike Masada, there is no cable car to carry the visitor to the summit, nor is the site thoroughly excavated. But the climb is not arduous from the east, and the remains of Herod's massive walls and cisterns are still to be seen on the site. As at all Herod's desert retreats, an ample water supply was essential to the fortress. The problem was resolved in two stages. In the sides of the mountain can be seen the great cisterns in which water was stored during the winter rains — similar low-level cisterns can be seen at Masada. Later, the water was transported in leather buckets to fill the cisterns within the fortress itself — a task involving thousands of slaves.

One event stands out in the history of this great stronghold. After the death of King Herod the Great in 4 B.C., his son Herod Antipas became ruler of Galilee and of the transjordanian territory called Peraea in which Machaerus stood. Antipas fell passionately for Herodias, his brother Philip's wife. (This was not the Philip who built Caesarea Philippi.) Antipas divorced his first wife, daughter of the Nabatean king, in order to marry Herodias.

Such events in the lives of the Herod dynasty were by no means unusual — Herod himself had ten wives. But the marriage of Antipas and Herodias attracted the condemnation of John the Baptist — the law of Moses prohibited such a marriage. Josephus tells how Antipas took his revenge by imprisoning John at Machaerus. But Herodias went further. The gospels tell how Salome, Herodias's daughter by Philip, danced before Antipas and then demanded of him as her reward the head of John the Baptist on a platter.

Later, like Masada, Machaerus was used as a retreat by the zealots as the Romans re-took the Holy Land at the end of the Jewish revolt. The fortress was destroyed by the Roman general Lucilius Bassus in A.D. 70 or 71. But it's worth reflecting that while Moses the greatest of the lawgivers died at Mount Nebo to the north, John the last of the prophets was executed here.

Return from Machaerus to the King's Highway.

The Wadi Mujib

The road going south soon comes to the magnificent Wadi Mujib — called the Arnon in the Old Testament. The road hardly begins to descend before coming to a lay-by where it is possible to stop to view this great canyon. Over the millennia, the winter rains have carved and fashioned the wadi into an extended landscape of unearthly hills and declivities in marl and shale, stratified, crumbled at the edges, capriciously piled up in one place and without prejudice gouged out viciously in another. The modern tarmac road spirals downwards into it descending from level to level for about five miles, then winds its way cautiously upwards on the other side.

So from time immemorial did the track of the King's Highway pass through the Arnon. In the eighteenth century B.C., the four kings of the north traversed the gorge with their armies. Five centuries later Moses led the Children of Israel in the opposite direction on their way to the promised land. After the arrival of the Israelites, the Arnon marked for a time the boundary between the territory of the tribe of Reuben and the kingdom of Moab.

The next stopping place is Kerak, about twenty miles to the south.

Kerak

Vast unwavering stretches of the transjordanian plateau are rarer south of the Wadi Mujib. Mostly the land is broken up. Kerak is piled untidily on reefs of rock suspended above deep ravines. Undulating hill country, punctuated only with the occasional plantation of olives, extends in all directions around the town. Despite the occasional modern building, Kerak itself is essentially mediaeval, a maze of winding streets and busy bazaars surmounted by the ruins of a vast Crusader castle. Yet this was a fortified city in Old Testament times. When it looked as though the Israelites would defeat him Mesha, king of Moab in the ninth century B.C., seeking divine assistance sacrificed his eldest son on the city walls.

Lunch at Kerak.

Drive into the town and turn along the main street called Sharia al-Qalaa. The castle is at the end of this street, and the Kerak Rest House stands to the right — probably the best restaurant on this route for a midday meal. After lunch, visit the remains of the castle, open from sunrise to sunset. No admission is charged but care should be taken — there are no handrails or restrictions to protect the visitor from the dangers of the site. Holes here and there invite a drop of thirty feet or so into the depths of some vaulted Crusader cavern.

In its heyday, this massive castle was designed to keep open the roads to Petra and Aqaba, and was manned by a garrison of thousands. It was built in 1132 by Payem the Butler, Lord of Transjordan, at the behest of Baldwin I, King of the Crusader Kingdom of Jerusalem. It was a shrewd move. From thenceforth, caravans of merchants moving along the trade route were obliged to pay tolls to their Crusader protectors — money poured into the coffers of the knights of Kerak. Not only that, but this was one of the main routes of the 'haj', the pilgrimage which all Muslims wish to make at least once in a lifetime to Mecca, the holy city of Islam. And the castle was important strategically. Baldwin would receive from Kerak warnings of an approaching enemy — a likely route for the invading armies of Islam. Beacons were used to exchange signals between Kerak and Jerusalem. And to the west on the shores of the Dead Sea, the Crusaders had built a small port to give quick access to the Judean hill country and Jerusalem itself.

Baldwin IV, a boy of thirteen suffering from leprosy, became king of the Crusader Kingdom of Jerusalem in 1174. For a time, Miles de Plancy, Lord of Transjordan, acted as his regent. But de Plancy was assassinated, leaving his wife Stephanie as ruler of Kerak. She was now one of the richest women in the Holy Land, a fact which attracted the attention of an unscrupulous knight named Reginald de Chatillon. Within a short time, he was master of Kerak, with Stephanie as his wife. Baldwin made a truce with Saladin, a move greatly to the advantage of Kerak for trade along the caravan route increased greatly. But the temptation was too great for de Chatillon. He seized a rich caravan heading for Mecca, a move which so incensed Saladin that he declared a 'jihad', a holy war, against the Crusaders. It led to the disastrous defeat of the Crusaders at the Horns of Hittim in 1187. Saladin treated the knights with courtesy after the battle, but he used his own sword to decapitate de Chatillon. Stephanie continued to rule Kerak until, in the following year, Saladin captured the castle.

The castle today still gives a good impression of the sheer size of this great Crusader fortress. Cavernous vaulted halls and vast crenellated defensive walls give evidence of the importance of the castle they called Crak which dominated the trade route for fifty years. An interesting museum is also to be found in the castle grounds. Nor has Christianity disappeared from the town. An uneasy relationship between the Christians and the Muslims of Kerak led to the Christian resettlement of Madaba in the nineteenth century — see p. 46. But there remain many old families living in Kerak whose allegiance to Christianity dates back to the Byzantine period.

Continue south on the King's Highway. Further interesting Crusader ruins can be seen at Tafila and at Shobak, illustrating the way in which the knights built a string of fortresses within easy proximity of each other. But about eighty-five miles separate Kerak from Petra and your time available for visiting them may be limited.

The Wadi Musa

Before arriving in Petra, the road passes through the Wadi Musa — 'Moses' spring'. The emergence of an abundant stream of clear water out of a large rock in the valley has reminded people of the biblical story in which Moses struck a rock and water flowed out for the Israelites to drink. Nowadays, this spring has been housed in a small, white, domed building at the roadside about a mile from Petra, the water is cool and fit for drinking.

Petra

The Petra Forum Hotel was opened in 1983 and is situated about a mile from the narrow cleft in the rocks — called the 'Siq' — which affords access to the remains of the great city itself. In the vicinity of the Siq is a small settlement of Jordanian houses and, about three miles away, a large bedouin settlement. Until recently the bedouins inhabited the caves in Petra itself but they have now been rehoused by the Jordanian government. The hills around the Rest House and the hotel are terraced and grow figs, vines and olives. The hotel is owned by the Jordanian government but is administered by the international chain of Forum Hotels. Cheaper alternative accommodation is available at the Petra Rest House, where the rooms are used as dormitories when there are many guests. Even if you are staying at the Forum, the Guest House is worth a visit — built to look like something from outer space, yet classical pillars grace the foyer. The Rest House was built incorporating the tomb called Al Khan. The name means caravanserai — perhaps there was once a camping ground for camel caravans nearby.

Look around the entrance to the Petra canyon in the cool of the evening. The terraced hillsides grow olives and almonds, figs and vines. The air is limpid and clear; birdsong abounds, interrupted only by the hooting of car horns so beloved of Jordanian taxi drivers.

Overnight at Petra.

Accommodation at Petra

Petra Forum Hotel, four star, Wadi Mousa, P.O. Box 30 (tel: 03-61246 or Amman 634200)

Petra Rest House, Wadi Mousa, P.O. Box Amman 2863 (tel: 03-83011)

KERAK: USEFUL INFORMATION

Population:	7,400
Altitude:	3,400 ft
Facilities:	rest house, Crusader castle

Allenby/Hussein Bridge 137 miles

PETRA: USEFUL INFORMATION

Facilities:	hotel, restaurants, unique remains of ancient city and acropolis

Queen Alia Airport 135 miles

The Garden Tomb at Petra

DAY 10

Petra, the rose-red city . . .

Early in the morning, walk or ride on a horse through the narrow crack called the Siq which runs through the mountains into Petra. At the end of it see the great tomb called the Treasury, so called because until recently the tribesmen of the region expected silver and gold to pour out of a stone urn high on the facade — if only their bullets could split it! Spend the day in this, the most remarkable of all archaeological sites, once the capital city of the mysterious Nabateans. It would take a fortnight to see it all, but a day is enough to experience something of the mystery immortalized in Dean Burgon's romantic phrase, 'a rose-red city half as old as time'. If permitted by your flight times it would be simplest to spend a second night at Petra before taking a taxi to the airport.

Petra

There are several clues to Petra. One is a saddle on a camel, depicted on a Nabatean coin.

Who were the Nabateans? From the dawn of time, bedouin tribes from the deserts of Arabia had intermittently descended on the centres of civilization in the Middle East. Uncivilized newcomers in a continuous chain destroyed cities and uprooted cultures. In the third millennium B.C., the Sumerian city states of the lower Mesopotamian valley were harassed by beer-swilling, imperialistic Akkadians. A thousand years later cities suffered from the wild razzias of the Amorites, the bad men of the Syrian deserts. So too did the Canaanite cities of the Holy Land suffer at the hands of the Israelites coming in out of the desert in the mid-thirteenth century B.C. The history of Jericho illustrates over and over again how great cities were destroyed by newcomers who lived in tents or holes in the ground. The inhabitants of the land in the region south of the Dead Sea in the sixth century B.C. were a people called Edomites. The Nabateans were the latest in a long line of desert newcomers. Like earlier predators, they appeared as if from nowhere.

Edom was an ancient kingdom — it is mentioned many times in the Old Testament. But it was also a land of great opportunities for acquiring wealth — because the trade routes of the Middle East passed this way. To control the trade routes required great military power. The Nabatean invention of the camel saddle afforded that kind of supremacy. Until this time, camels were ungainly animals which were difficult to ride. But the Nabateans created a wooden-framed camel saddle which could be placed over the hump. The camel suddenly became a fast and flexible form of transport, and transformed the Nabateans into a military power dominating the trade routes from Arabia to Egypt, from Aqaba to Damascus. The Edomites were largely ousted from their land, although they reappear in the New Testament period as Idumeans.

It's worth being taken around Petra by a guide. When you arrive outside the Treasury, you will be offered a choice of routes around the remains of the city, depending on how much time you are prepared to spend there. For a one-day visit, choose to climb to the 'high place of sacrifice' — this too is an important clue to the mysteries of Petra. But first examine the great classical-style tomb itself — it has a facade as high as Nelson's column and a cavernous interior

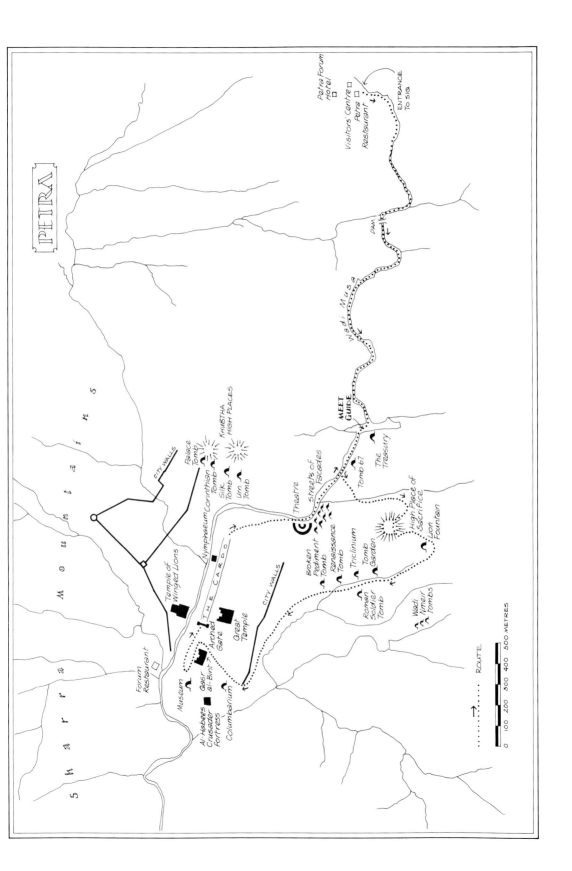

PETRA

Sharra Mountains

Forum Restaurant

Museum
Al-Habees
Crusader Fortress
Qasr al-Bint?
Columbarium
Arched Gate
THE CARDO
Great Temple
CITY WALLS
Temple of Winged Lions
Nymphaeum
CITY WALLS
Palace Tomb
Corinthian Tomb
Silk Tomb
Urn Tomb
Khubtha High Places

Theatre
Streets of Facades
Broken Pediment Tomb
Renaissance Tomb
Triclinium
Tomb Garden
Roman Soldier Tomb
Wadi Nmeir Tombs
Lion Fountain
High Place of Sacrifice
Tomb 61
The Treasury
MEET GUIDE

Wadi Musa

DAM

Patra Forum Hotel
Visitors Centre
Petra Restaurant
ENTRANCE TO SIQ

· · · · · · ROUTE

0 100 200 300 400 500 METRES

leading into several burial compartments. Notice the artistry with which the masons who carved this tomb out of the rock utilized the veins of different colour in the sandstone, ranging from purple to yellow. After seeing the Treasury, climb into the hills with your guide to see the 'high place'. It stands about seven hundred feet above the city, and takes about twenty-five minutes to get there through the Wadi Mahafir. But notice that the Nabateans afforded access to their holy place with rock-cut staircases.

Just below the 'high place', you will see two pillars over twenty feet high which were created by cutting away the ridge around them. Such pillars were common among all the religions of the ancient Middle East, usually related to the fertility of crops, flocks and wives — when they arrived in the Holy Land, the Israelites were instructed to raise stone pillars on Mount Ebal in the hill country and to inscribe on them the Ten Commandments.

High places, too, are mentioned many times in the Old Testament, execrated by the later prophets because their rituals were associated with the religion of the Canaanites. Yet in concept the temple built by Solomon on the apex of the ridge in Jerusalem was not very different from the great stepped temples of Mesopotamia or, indeed, from this high place at Petra. The shrine of the god and the altar of sacrifice to propitiate the god stood at the apex of a great structure. On the high place at Petra, you will see that the worshippers faced a raised platform — evidently the shrine of the god. And to the left of the platform is an altar of sacrifice complete with a circular basin from which a drain runs away carrying the blood of the animal — a maze of such drains has been found through the sacred rock under the Dome of the Rock at Jerusalem, where the Altar of Sacrifice of the Temple once stood.

We know relatively little of the religion of the Nabateans and, indeed, this high place may have been inherited by them from the Edomites. But it is clear that the cult was of great importance to the citizens of ancient Petra. They probably came here to sacrifice to the god of the mountain they called Dhu-Sharra. Very likely an image of the god occupied the shrine, in contrast with the empty room of the Holy of Holies, in Jerusalem.

A little to the north of this high place, but inaccessible to the visitor, are the remains of a shrine to the moon. This again reminds the visitor of a unique characteristic of the religion of Israel — the Israelites believed in one God and in no other.

146

Before leaving the high place, look at the great basin itself in which Petra was built — to the north hang the Sharra mountains, named after the god Dhu-Sharra. The city was a fortress completely enclosed by mountains on the edge of the Arabah, few places were more inaccessible to an enemy. When Herod the Great was fleeing from the Parthians in 40 B.C., he sought refuge in Petra — it was refused. But there are much earlier biblical associations with this scene. Away to the left is the mountain on which can be found the tomb of Aaron, the high priest who was Moses' brother and who shared the task of leading the Israelites out of Egypt. The Muslim inhabitants of today continue to revere 'the tomb of Haroun'.

Descend from the high place by the longer route through the Wadi Farasa. Nabatean inscriptions appear on the rocks. The Nabateans were illiterate when they arrived from the desert in the sixth century B.C., but by the late fourth century B.C. they had adapted to their use the Aramaic script common in the Middle East of the time. A little further down is one of the civic treasures of Petra — a huge rock-carved lion through which water once spouted out of its mouth. Perhaps the worshippers on their way to the high place stopped for refreshments at this elegant fountain.

The tombs of Petra proliferate as you descend — yet another clue to the mysteries of this city. There are many small tombs, little more than shafts cut into the cliff face; but there are also extended vistas of great tombs in classical or oriental styles. Nowhere in the Holy Land has so much labour and so much artistry gone into the creation of burial places as at Petra. In comparison, Herod's family tomb in Jerusalem or even the so-called Tomb of Absolom in the Valley of the Kidron, pale into insignificance. Only the tombs of the pharoahs supersede these.

But why did the Nabateans go to such lengths when it came to their tombs? As with other aspects of Petra, the answer is almost certainly to be found in the world of the ancient Middle East in general. The archaeologists have found many forms of burial, all of them related to religion — although it is not always possible to decide what exactly people believed. Different types of burial were found, for instance, among the early cave dwellers of the Carmel Range. At one time bodies were buried flexed, their heads decorated with beads — preparation perhaps for a triumphant entry into a world beyond the grave. The nomads of the Golan created dolmens for their dead — some kind of ante-rooms to the underworld. And not unlike the tombs of the pharoahs, the rock-cut tombs at Jericho in the late Canaanite period were stocked with provisions, as it were for a journey. If the deity of the Nabateans at Petra was Dhu-Sharra, the god of the mountain, it is likely that they expected their dead to enter into eternity within the mountain itself.

It's worth bearing in mind that comparatively little archaeological excavation has gone on at Petra — soundings have been taken in a few places but that is all. As you enter the floor of the basin visit the city centre where you will see the remains of temples, markets, a nymphaeum and a colonnaded street reminiscent of Jerash (see p. 50). These too help the visitor to understand the city. The Romans ruled Petra, certainly. In A.D. 106 the emperor Trajan ordered the Roman governor of Syria to conquer the Nabateans — the effect was to create the new Roman province of Arabia. But Petra was at the apex of its prosperity at about the time of Christ, long before the Roman invasion. The great public buildings of the city centre were not built by the Romans, but by the Nabateans. They created a great fortress city of about thirty thousand inhabitants, dedicated to the god of the mountain, classical in style and surrounded by a great necropolis also classical in style. Visit the museum, not only to study the artifacts of Nabatean and Roman Petra which are on display, but as you leave to see also the city centre from the best possible vantage point. This is the very heart of Petra. It is not enough simply to visit the site — one must also envisage the great city that was here.

As you return through the Siq at the end of your visit to Petra, look at the surface of the rocks about twelve feet above ground level. Here and there, you will see the remains of clay pipes embedded in the rock face — you will have seen similar water pipes in the museum at Hazor. They too are an important clue to this city. Clear springs of water, such as were found in the countryside around Petra, were piped and brought into the city through the Siq to transform the desert fortress into a paradise of civic gardens and fountains. The Nabateans may have originated as uncivilized desert tribes, but they also created a civilization of great complexity and sophistication.

Our tour of the Holy Land ends here; ideally your schedule will allow you to devote a complete day to exploring Petra and remain a second night before leaving for the airport.

Overnight at Petra.

Bar within a tomb at the Petra Rest House

Transliterate Arabic

There is little need to be able to read Hebrew script when following this itinerary. In the State of Israel and the occupied territories, nearly all signs are in Hebrew, Arabic and English. The situation is different, however, in the Hashemite Kingdom of Jordan where signs are often in Arabic only.

To western eyes, the swirls and dots which make up written Arabic may seem at first intractable. But the writing system like ours is alphabetic, if organized in a different way from our script.

Arabic is written from right to left — books and magazines begin on what to us would be the back page.

There are no capital letters.

With the exception of the first letter 'alif', all Arabic letters are consonants.

In English, the printed form has been developed out of the nucleus of the cursive form of a letter; _h_ , for instance, is printed **h** .

Such ligatures are common in cursive English — a small case 'h' for instance is often written _the_ , linking the letter to other letters within a word. _the_ Flourishes are also added _Rec_

Unlike the style used for printed English, Arabic words even in print are always cursive — the letters, with certain exceptions, joined to each other by ligatures.

The nucleus ﺱ, for instance, gives the sound 's' as in sit, to which can be added a ligature before ﺳ and after ﺴ. A final flourish is also added ﺲ

Some of the letters in the Arabic alphabet have their equivalents in English — others do not.

sound	nucleus	with flourishes and ligatures
a (or alif)	ا	no ligatures
b as in English	ب	ﺒ
t as in English	ت	ﺘ
th as in 'thing'	ث	ﺜ
j as in English	ج	ﺠ
H from the back of the throat	ح	ﺤ
kh as in 'loch'	خ	ﺨ
d as in English	د	ﺪ
dh as in 'that'	ذ	ﺬ
r as in 'marrow'	ر	ﺮ
z as in English	ز	ﺰ

151

s as in 'sit'	س	سـ
sh as in English	ش	شـ
S more open mouthed than in English	ص	صـ
D more open mouthed than in English	ض	ضـ
T more open mouthed than in English	ط	طـ
DH a sibilant zh	ظ	ظـ
: violent glottal stop — gõ-it	ع	ـعـ
gh a bit like a French rolled 'r'	غ	ـغـ
f as in English	ف	فـ
q a hard 'k'	ق	قـ
k as in English	ك	كـ
l as in English	ل	لـ

m
as in English

n
as in English

h
as in 'hat'

w
as in English

y
as in English

hamza
glottal stop — gõ-it

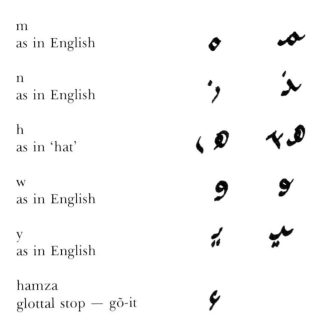

Double consonants are sounded twice

While a great deal more could be said about written Arabic, I hope that there is enough information here to enable you to read road signs etc. The main rule is to look for the nucleus of each letter.

Index of places

OTHER TITLES IN THIS SERIES

TRAVELS IN ALSACE & LORRAINE
TRAVELS IN BRITTANY
TRAVELS IN BURGUNDY
TRAVELS IN THE DORDOGNE
TRAVELS IN THE LOIRE
TRAVELS IN NORMANDY
TRAVELS IN PROVENCE
TRAVELS IN TUSCANY

All the titles offer the reader a ten/fourteen day journey through the region pointing out places of interest, hotels and restaurants, with special emphasis on the food and wines of the area. Each book also contains a mapped itinerary with distances and times for each day of the journey.

As well as hints and tips on what to buy and eat in the region, readers are provided with a selection of recipes and menus to enjoy on their return.

All titles now available from bookshops. In case of difficulty, please contact Merehurst Limited, Ferry House, 51-57 Lacy Road, Putney, London SW15 1PR, telephone 01-780 1177.